GRACIOUS INTERIORS

GRACIOUS INTERIORS

Mary Kelly Selover

MetroBooks

MetroBooks

An Imprint of Friedman/Fairfax Publishers

Library of Congress Cataloging-in-Publication Data

Selover, Mary Kelly.
    Gracious interiors/Mary Kelly Selover.
        p.   cm.
Includes bibliographical references and index.
ISBN 1-56799-173-4
1. Interior decoration — Handbooks, manuals, etc.   I. Title.
NK2115.S42   1995
747.2—dc20   95-3070
                                                       CIP

Editor: Susan Lauzau
Art Director: Jeff Batzli
Designers: Andrea Karman and Jennifer Markson
Photography Editor: Colleen A. Branigan
Production Manager: Jeanne E. Hutter

Color separations by Ocean Graphic International Company Ltd.
Printed in China by Leefung-Asco Printers Ltd.

For bulk purchases and special sales, please contact:
Friedman ⁄ Fairfax Publishers
Attention: Sales Department
15 West 26th Street
New York, NY 10010
212⁄685-6610 FAX 212⁄685-1307

Visit the Friedman Fairfax Website:
http://www.webcom.com/friedman

To my father,
whose love of
the written word
and innate good taste
(except in wallpaper)
continue to inspire...

CONTENTS

INTRODUCTION

For most of us, decorating a home has become an expensive proposition. Few can afford to remodel a house or an apartment all at once; today's budgets often demand that improvements be made one room at a time. This volume has, in fact, been organized to reflect that reality. Each chapter is devoted to a single kind of room or space—from entryways to living rooms to baths to sunrooms and more. By grouping together a range of treatments and solutions for a room's dilemmas, the design possibilities are shown to be limitless.

And each chapter embraces numerous styles, including American country, English country, Arts and Crafts, Southwest, postmodern, neoclassical, Victorian, and eclectic. This book is intended as a resource for those hoping to discover the aesthetic that best suits them as well as for those who are already certain of stylistic preference yet searching for worthy examples to emulate and ideas to borrow.

Because this year's catchy concept can easily become next year's expensive cliché, the spaces showcased here have been selected at least in part for their enduring appeal. However, interiors that stand the test of time are not necessarily traditional or formal settings. Rooms with staying power can be contemporary and casual, too, though most share the elements of timeless design: singular vision, appropriateness for the space, and genuine comfort.

Besides illustrating through photographs the wonderful work of many talented designers, the book strives to edify. The captions have been written to provide insight about the decisions that shaped the design of each space rather than merely to describe what the reader can readily ascertain. In fact, the book is purposely caption-oriented rather than discursive, in order to provide the most useful, concrete information.

Presumably, time-starved readers—of which there are many—will turn first to the chapter that includes the kind of room they next wish to decorate. Then they'll look at

Opposite: This mahogany, scroll-shaped sleigh bed with square plinth feet and scallop-shell carving inspired the early-nineteenth-century empire theme that defines the room. Heavy curtain rods with gilded finials and rings suggest the ormolu mounts common to furnishings of this period. The curtains and checkerboard coverlet are refreshing contemporary touches. The bedside table is inspired by bookshelves designed by famed decorator Billy Baldwin.

the photographs, reading the captions to learn which elements make the room successful from a design perspective. If in the near future they plan to make a purchase, be it a piece of upholstered furniture or a ceiling fan, they will read the appropriate boxed text for practical particulars. Finally, they will turrn to the chapter introduction for background information and guidance.

Whether you read *Gracious Interiors* straight through or piece by piece, you'll find that effort has been made to present design styles and decorating tips in an accessible way. Just because the book is beautiful, don't let it languish on a coffee table. Mark the pages you like and the captions that offer advice pertinent to your problems. And scribble a few notes inside the back cover. In this way, the book will become the best guide to creating your very own gracious interiors.

Opposite: Red walls make the mantelpiece and moldings in this comfortable home real standouts. Worn armchairs come to life courtesy of chintz slipcovers trimmed with cording and fringe. An inexpensive particleboard table is draped with the same fabric, then crowned with an old openwork cloth found at a garage sale. Cut crystal, here in the form of a lamp, makes a sophisticated sidekick to a small collection of majolica-style pottery. Other pieces stand opposite platters, cachepots, and a teacup in an ever-popular blue and white pattern.

Left: A vivid imagination combines with strong, clear colors, wrought-iron accessories, and religious icons to create this arresting folkloric dining room. Sawtooth wood trim skirts a plain pine table and tops a folding screen. The chair rail is painted in place.

Chapter One

ENTRYWAYS

Opposite: Luxurious fabrics dress up the entry to this cozy cottage. Windows are treated to swagged valances and kerchief-style curtains; an old table is draped with a deeply fringed skirt. This spot, with its nontraditional bay, may be used for breakfast or for a leisurely cup of afternoon tea. The walls and dutch door, sponged a deep green, and a cool stone floor contribute to the space's outdoor feeling. The carved wooden piece above the door and the timeworn putti bust playfully evoke garden accents.

nticipation. No matter what the style or decor of the home, this is the feeling every foyer, vestibule, or entry should stir. Usually smaller in size—but not necessarily in stature—than a residence's other rooms, this space speaks temptingly of what is to come. Besides providing an introduction into the home, this threshold should also serve as a comfortable place for visitors and family members to pause and put aside the cares of the workaday world. The entryway is the point of passage into the home—and metaphorically into the life—of the family.

In most cases, it's desirable for the decoration of the entryway to be in keeping with the period and character of the rest of the house. In particular, flooring should complement the treatments found underfoot in adjacent rooms. Wood, brick, tile, granite, marble, flagstone, terrazzo, concrete, vinyl, and rubber are all materials that can be used successfully for entry floors. Since the entryway is by definition a high traffic area, subject to heavy wear as well as mud and grime from the outdoors, carpeting is not the best option for this space. Rugs, however, when placed atop a washable, durable surface, make a wonderful choice, providing additional warmth, texture, pattern, and color. What's more, rugs can easily be rolled up and removed for home or professional cleaning.

Just as the floor in the entryway must be able to withstand daily trampings, so, too, should the walls be able to endure their share of scratches and bruises. When selecting paint for the entry, consider durability and opt for a paint with a somewhat glossy finish rather than one that is strictly matte. Glossies wipe clean of fingerprints and accumulated grime most readily. In addition, paints with gloss reflect more light, another plus for entries, which tend to be somewhat dark. Wallpaper used in entryways should be of the wipeable variety—even the most careful homeowners will find that marks have mysteriously appeared over time. Remember, too, to select a wall treatment that will serve as a foil for the accents, be they few or many, that decorate the entryway.

Because entryways don't generally offer an abundance of natural light, the choice and placement of fixtures are important. Floor space is usually at a premium, so overhead fixtures, table lamps, and wall sconces make excellent choices. An overhead light can create the illusion of more space but, when used as the sole source of illumination, can cast a harsh, unflattering glare. To avoid this problem, have the overhead fixture wired to a dimmer switch. Table lamps make a good secondary light source, as do sconces, which provide dramatic uplighting and are an inspired choice for entryways with beautiful moldings or ceilings. Picture lights and recessed lighting can fill in unattractive dark spots as well as direct attention to decorative pieces.

In its role as a "preview" space, the entry is ideal for displaying artwork and other collected items that offer insight into the rest of the home's personality. Treasured breakables, however, are best shown in other rooms where they are less likely to be endangered by delivery people, rambunctious children, and wayward pets. Furniture, to be practical, should be able to handle some wear and tear, and should be useful as well as decorative. If at all possible, create a place where packages can be set down momentarily, and provide a place to sit. Sideboards, benches, tables, and chairs usually suit these purposes and should be selected in scale with the entry. Pieces that are too small will make the space feel cavernous and unwelcoming, while furniture that is too large for the area will appear awkward and in the way.

Most importantly, an entryway should usher guests into your home with warmth and promise. A sense of pleasure and ease of passage are, after all, the qualities that ultimately enhance the feeling of any entryway.

Opposite: The elliptical fanlight and its sidelights dominate in the broad center hall of this Adams-style house. In keeping with the eighteenth-century architecture, elaborate stenciling echoes the circular leaded glass pattern of the door. Above, a simple electrified lantern casts a warm glow over a drop-leaf table and worn but wonderful antique Oriental carpets.

Left: An antique Victorian bamboo hat rack serves as a useful repository for hats, scarves, coats, and other accessories. It's a convenient alternative to a small, cluttered closet. An old, partially stained and worn quilt has been given a new life as a rocker cushion cover. Although seemingly at odds stylistically, these furnishings work well together because of the casual way they have been accessorized and the pared-down nature of the rest of the entry.

Left: Rendered in sky blue, the faux finish of this vaulted ceiling has a celestial quality. This unusual treatment transcends the overall formality of the entry and its furnishings. Pale yellow sponged walls complement the gilt console table and the brass and crystal chandelier, as well as permit the dark-painted panels to appear brighter.

Above: No mere mudroom, the back entry to this contemporary home makes a welcoming conversation area, thanks to its cleverly constructed fireplace and built-in sofa with display niche. Contiguous to the kitchen, wood flooring runs throughout and complements the granite countertops. A small patio with a work area for pruning plants is just beyond the steel-and-glass doors.

Opposite: Angles, arches, stairs, and sky-lights create excitement in this entry with a two-story ceiling. Wooden shelves are topped with a whimsical pediment, and a wall with a plaster niche is painted with a subtle horizontal stripe. Both are filled with collected pieces of folk art. Wooden flooring, which leads to the living room, also infuses this space with warmth.

Right: The open-air entry of this home exemplifies Neoclassical restraint. Awash in soft ombré shades, the painted walls and terra-cotta tiled floor form a muted backdrop for a richly colored, exactingly carved Mediterranean-style side table, two petite leather-seated chairs, and carefully selected Greek and Roman antiquities. Through the double-height French doors, the living room awaits.

Left: This back entryway has been remodeled into a versatile screen-door sanctuary by some savvy homeowners. A built-in bench serves as a chaise longue and provides ample additional storage. Nesting tables, found for a pittance, have been repainted to coordinate with the William Morris–style wall covering. Underfoot, easy-care vinyl runs through to the kitchen.

MAKING SENSE OF WALL COVERINGS

No single element of a room has more impact than the wall covering. Its color and pattern set the tone, and wall coverings are available in a plethora of styles and period looks.

Today, most wall coverings are either vinyl coated or solid vinyl, which marks the word wallpaper *a misnomer. But before making a selection, it's wise to understand a few terms.*

◆ *Peelable The top layer of this wall covering strips away without steaming or scraping and leaves only a thin residue of paper or paste behind.*

◆ *Strippable This wall covering can be completely removed without steaming or scraping.*

◆ *Scrubbable Designed to be cleaned with a soft brush and mild detergent, this wall covering is great for kitchens and other high-maintenance areas.*

◆ *Washable This wall covering can be cleaned with a sponge and mild soap and water.*

Wall coverings can also aid in making tiny rooms appear more spacious and large rooms seem cozier. Following are some ideas about how to create the effect you want in your rooms.

SMALL ROOMS
To make a low ceiling appear higher, install a border about twenty-eight inches (71cm) above the floor (lower than normal chair rail height).

A dense, flowing pattern used on the walls and ceiling can help make a small room appear larger. A light background, wide stripes, or a vertical pattern can also help.

Cool colors, such as blue and green, create the illusion of size. Deep tones, such as red, tend to enclose a room, fostering an intimate effect.

LARGE ROOMS
A wide border around the ceiling will make a too-tall ceiling appear lower. It will also help to bring the room in scale with standard-size furniture and accessories.

To make a large room feel more intimate, try a bold design on the walls rather than opting for a dainty pattern.

Above: A sinuous banister, curved slate-covered steps, and stainless-steel risers and balusters come together to create a marvelous modern staircase in an entry. Solid oak flooring laid in traditional herringbone style offers pattern and color without detracting from the space's simplicity.

Below: The wrought-iron balustrade sets a fanciful mood in this entry-way. Prints and a mirror, all in gilt frames, are grouped to echo the angle of the stairway's ascent. Just below sits a painted cupboard, selected to match the color found in the pattern of the tiled stairs' risers. It is home to a collection of objects, both frivolous and fine. These are rotated by season, displayed on the cupboard's top and stored below.

Opposite: A Chippendale-style mirror with a soft white finish makes a less formal statement than would one with a gilded frame. The side chair is equally subtle. Both now complement rather than compete with the exceptional dentil molding over the door and the wonderful wainscoting in this stylish foyer.

Right: Elegant metal accessories in black give an edge to the entry and living room of this country house finished with simple bead-and-groove paneling and polished wood floors. An oversize mirror makes another bold stroke. When hanging a mirror, be certain to determine what it will reflect before sinking the nail. After all, most rooms have at least one flaw; it's wise not to "double" it.

 *Above:* Stained a striking blue, the floor of this spare entry with landing promises more surprises to come. For a space this simple to look its best, all the painted finishes, including baseboard and window trim, must be pristine.

Above: This Spanish Colonial Revival home boasts a terra-cotta tiled entry and a beautiful arched board-and-batten door fitted with ornate iron hardware. Old-world touches include a cascading curtain, which can be drawn across the threshold, and a multidrop crystal chandelier. Rough-hewn yet elegantly proportioned, the sideboard not only complements the door's color but provides compromise between contrasting design elements.

Above: A dramatic circular entry is made even more so thanks to boldly painted walls and a marble floor in a classic checkerboard pattern. Strong colors can be used in entryways of almost any size without fear of creating a claustrophobic feeling. Family members and visitors seldom spend more than a few minutes in this space, so give in to brillant creative urges.

Above: Standard pegboard is a most ingenious way to display this assortment of shadowboxes, pictures, and a quilt. What's more, items can be repositioned and other pieces used or removed without having to hide or repair unsightly nail holes. A pair of brackets and a narrow piece of glass have been used to create a spot for potted plants as well as to enhance the three-dimensional effect of the grouping.

Opposite: The homeowner's passion for all things handcrafted envelops those who enter this lovingly renovated two-story residence. When grouping objects for an unstudied display, first choose those that share attributes, including color, shape, or purpose. Next, add pieces that offer contrast in texture, size, and degree of detail.

Above: Deep blue walls set off this collection of porcelain and pottery. The molding has been painted a bright white for exceptional contrast. An oak sideboard has a single wide drawer fitted inside with organizers to hold cleaning receipts, warranties for products, and spare keys. Rush-weave side chairs have colorful polished chintz cushions with welt trim.

Chapter Two

LIVING ROOMS

Opposite: Reproduction furnishings in a variety of styles come together in every part of this newly built home. The room is full of contrasting textures—velvet, wood, metal, glass, ceramic, and stucco. Successfully achieving an eclectic aesthetic such as this takes considerable practice. Begin by assembling mismatched pieces that have something in common—color, material, or theme. Then experiment by introducing pieces in contrasting textures and hues to see if you like the look.

*O*nce designated the drawing room, later baptized the parlor, and today labeled the living room, this space has changed dramatically over time. The metamorphosis has occurred as manners and lifestyles have become more informal. But rather than making this room easier to decorate, this relaxing of standards has posed difficulties for many people. Some have chosen to ignore the changes, creating little-used shrines to a bygone era. Others have readily embraced all that is casual, turning these living spaces into anything-goes rumpus rooms.

First and foremost, today's living room should be a comfortable place for conversation with family members and guests alike. Secondly, it should be the scene for entertainments such as listening to music, watching television, and reading. Because all of these activities are pursued while sitting, selecting chairs and sofas and deciding on their placement is critical. Even in formal rooms replete with period furniture, there are ways to include comfortable upholstered pieces that serve neutral but necessary roles. A living room without several pleasurable places to plunk down will be depressingly empty of people.

More pieces of upholstered furniture are used in the living room than in any other room of the house. For this reason, fabrics will predominate here. Whatever its style, the living room provides the optimum opportunity to use lovely fabrics. Remember that the duty of living room fabrics is to help create a cocoon of comfort. Velvet and brocade, damask and silk—all are appropriate here when selected with judgment and some restraint. Polished cotton, wool, linen, and certain blends can look nearly as luxurious. When deciding on a fabric for furniture, remember that reupholstering is not only expensive, it stresses chair and sofa frames. To protect an investment in good furniture, buy the best that your budget will allow. Quality fabric will last longer and inevitably look better than cheaper stuff.

Curtains warrant the same advice: money is better spent on fine materials and careful construction than on elaborate design. Curtains should be pretty, never pretentious. The architecture of the windows, as well as their height and width, and the style of the furnishings in the room offer the surest guides for choosing a curtain style.

The layout of any living room should be determined by its focal point. This is generally the fireplace or the television and stereo, preferably housed in a cabinet of some kind. Ignoring the room's true focus will lead to errors in furniture selection and an uncomfortable arrangement, resulting in a stuffy and stilted room.

Unlike the dining room or the bedroom, the living room seldom has large pieces of furniture directly in its center. By default, color, pattern, and texture underfoot become more important here. Depending on the style of the space, almost any material that will stand up to anticipated wear and resist stains is suitable. Think of the floor as a fifth and dominant wall. It's a worthwhile way to learn how the floor treatment can best contribute to the beauty and visual balance of the living room.

As the true heart of the home, the living room is the premier space for entertaining guests and relaxing with family. Whether your living room is formal or casual, country Victorian or upscale modern, follow your own instincts and tastes; a room that genuinely pleases you will undoubtedly please those close to you, too.

Opposite: This newly constructed Arts and Crafts–style home has been decorated with a purist's enthusiasm for the period. Stickley furnishings, both antique pieces and those made today, are used throughout. A Tiffany-style ceiling fixture and table lamp radiate color as well as light. Underfoot, a subtly patterned rug picks up these hues. As was the fashion in the late nineteenth century, the oil painting hangs from the molding that runs at door height throughout the living room.

Left: Sumptuous seating holds sway in this space with its rolled-arm Victorian settee, plumped with an assortment of luxurious pillows, and a wide window seat made comfy with a fluffy bolster. The room's walls have been sponged in two distinct patterns and tones to suggest a wainscot. Note the way the exposed pipe, painted gold, recedes against this glowing backdrop. A small caned bench used as an occasional table, a wooden folding chair, and a Victorian bamboo side table combine to exude a solarium sensibility that works well with the mullioned windows.

Opposite: French flavor permeates this living room with its painted, caned-back bergère chairs, beautiful stone mantle, and strong, sloping chimney. The bookcases have been carefully designed to mimic the arches above the transom-topped windows. The small table is a perfect spot for a game of backgammon or dinner à deux. A single fabric in a linen stripe and a warm sisal rug complete the tranquil statement.

Right, top: Beautiful paneled walls and a lovely tulip chintz with "tea-stained" background create a genteel air in this apartment. Colorful geometric-patterned pillows and cranberry piping on the upholstered pieces, plus the roman shade in cotton, add extra punch. The tole tray table and the circular walnut Biedermeier-style table are reproductions. Prints selected for the wall share an outdoor theme although their frames sport varying finishes. Mismatched brackets offer another interesting way to display unlike objects.

Right, bottom: Paneling, in this instance a knotty pine, plays a preeminent role in this space reminiscent of an English drawing room. The serpentine valance frames a lovely bay window fitted with a plump plaid loveseat. A low, black lacquer table provides color balance for the baby grand and, along with the lamps and pieces of porcelain, some Chinese export influence. Chairs, like the loveseat, are skirted; the low-pile rug is contrastingly tailored.

Above: In the living room of a small apartment, it's wise to keep the arrangement flexible. In this instance the mostly contemporary furnishings are in their "everyday" positions. Except for the marquetry sideboard, all are artfully arranged on the diagonal to create two conversation areas. When the owner throws a cocktail party, the center of the space can be opened by placing the pieces closer to the room's perimeter.

Opposite: The Empire-style secretary and commode in this living room immediately announce its masculine bearing. Neoclassical accents include a Greek key ceiling border, architectural prints, and a pair of ormolu-style table lamps. Billowy silk taffeta curtains and the Oriental carpet with ivory field are on the lighter side. By design, the rest of the furniture is Art Deco–inspired.

Above: Bright white walls give this room its open feeling despite an awkward doorway. Plaid club chairs and a tufted ottoman are masculine but not too massive. The sofa, slipcovered in a cotton duck and piped in navy, is slouchy yet sophisticated. Note the beautiful parquet floor laid on the diagonal and topped with a rag rug. All the elements here are both easy to live with and easy to maintain.

Above: Color gives character to the small narrow living room of this apartment, with the reds of the wool dhurrie rug acting as the departure point for the scheme. The painted walls and the pair of sofas are a near-perfect match. The lighter toile and the checked slipcover fabric prevent the room from becoming oversaturated with this shade. Wooden elements, including two reproduction tables and the curtain rod and rings, give some needed gloss. What's more, it's wise to keep the treatment simple when the windows are less than stunning.

Opposite: Like dollops of paint from a modern artist's palette, velvets and damasks in eye-popping shades make flattering foils in this mostly monochromatic room. The white sofa, with its nail heads exposed, is a standout as is the custom-made area rug. Accent pieces, including the chair, coffee table, and lamp, are basically black.

Below: Horizontally striped sheers obscure the view but embrace the light in this living room with enviably high ceilings. The chesterfield sofa and high-backed armchair lend a nostalgic air. Serving as a coffee table, the ottoman is draped with a spare yard of silk damask. The contemporary slipper chair is notable for its comfortably wide seat; a sisal rug keeps the space neutral and leaning toward the natural.

Right: Color as well as style recalls the Art Deco period in this carefully designed living room. Combined with creamy white walls, ocher makes a strong statement. The silky velvet sofa and smooth, low-pile carpeting are exceedingly luxuriant. Coffee tables in shapes reminiscent of musical notes as well as other sensuously curved pieces are all harmonious Jazz Age elements.

CHOOSING UPHOLSTERED FURNITURE

When shopping for upholstered furniture, keep in mind the three F's: frame, filling, and fabric.

◆ *Frame A frame made of a hardwood with a dense grain, such as ash, maple, walnut, or oak, and frames that have been kiln-dried (so they won't later warp) are your best bets. The frame joints should be secured with dowels and glue rather than nails or screws; wood on wood makes the strongest connection. A good frame should not wobble or creak. Check the "pressure points," such as where the legs meet the seat bottom. Also, try to determine whether these areas have been reinforced with corner blocks.*

◆ *Filling The longevity and comfort of a sofa lies in its springs. Eight-way hand-tied coil springs (individual springs secured to the frame in eight places) provide the best—and most expensive—support. The mid-range option offers prefabricated springs inserted into the frame. Least expensive and least comfortable are side-by-side zigzag wires that support the cushions.*

In cushions, quality can be measured by density. Options include all down, a foam center wrapped with down, a mixture of down and synthetic fiberfill, or fiberfill alone.

◆ *Fabric Make sure that the pattern on seat-cushion fronts lines up with the rest of the sofa. Look for tight, neat, sturdy tailoring. Welts should be even; skirts should be lined. Feel all around the piece to make sure that padding is plentiful, especially on the arms and back where wear will be heavy. If the fabric isn't protected from the frame, it can show through in time.*

Opposite: Positioning the sofa in front of the fireplace could have created a poor traffic pattern via the adjacent doorway. The best solution: put the sofa in front of the picture window. Although this placement exaggerates the length and narrowness of the room, the dimensions are counterbalanced by the high, sloping ceiling. The glass-topped coffee table enhances the openness of the room's center. Artwork is creatively hung on the bookshelves as well as the walls.

Right: Spare but not bare, this living room is a work in progress. Floors have been bleached and pickled, and make-do furnishings are covered with yards of muslin. Salvaged column and pilaster have found a new but not yet permanent home. Keeping the color scheme completely monochromatic brings disparate elements together and demonstrates a purpose and plan. It's one of the easiest ways to make more of less.

Above: Viewed from behind the glazed-tile counter of the kitchen's passthrough, the living room and dining area form a soothing sea of blues and greens. The focal point is the contemporary fireplace. Eschewing a more formal mantlepiece, a simple glass shelf has been installed instead. An eclectic mix of wooden furnishings, some of Middle Eastern extraction, speak of the homeowners' interest in foreign travel and lend an exotic air to the room.

Below: An arc of brushed stainless steel creates a mantlepiece as well as a storage place for logs. The hearth, like the bracketed shelf, is crafted of marble. Bleached and stained a soft silvery shade, the wood floor runs throughout the downstairs rooms.

Above: Right down to its curved fender, this fireplace is an exquisite example of Art Nouveau design. The mantlepiece is lovingly carved and scrolled; the accessories and triptych oil painting have been carefully chosen to complement rather than overpower the mantle, which serves as the room's focal point.

Opposite: Shards of ceramic tile create a striking hearth and surround designed by a talented artisan. On either side of this handsome fireplace, mullioned-door bookcases provide dust-free display.

Below: The original surround for this Mission-style mantlepiece has been replaced with one of ruddy limestone. A plaid rolled-arm chair and the antique lamp's leather shade repeat the hue.

Above: The fish came first, then came the idea for the blue and white harlequin-style fireplace surround in this summer home. Expert tile cutting was required to make sure the execution was flawless. For any tile project, work out the design very carefully on paper. Then, measure once, twice, thrice.

Opposite: Italian in feeling, this tiny arched fireplace has been subtly painted a chalky blue and its minimal trim painted and rubbed with gold. Using faux painting techniques, the walls were then sponged. Tiles, fabrics, and accessories share their burnished tones.

Above: The sofa might be swayed back, but there's nothing laid-back about this high-style contemporary living room. Silk taffeta curtains puddling on the floor, upholstered mannequins appearing as sculpture, and a free-form area rug all contribute to the riot of color. The pony-skin chair and coffee table make pivotal points in black.

Right: Against a nearly neutral background, a pair of modern paintings takes center stage. Twin hassocks in nonmatching blues and an emerald green sofa have been placed at sharp right angles. Throughout the space, all is strictly modern except for the traditional marble fireplace cluttered with handcrafted religious icons.

Opposite: It's no mystery which chair is his and which is hers in the perfectly symmetrical sitting area of this large living room. Fine antiques, Oriental carpets, and luxurious fabrics create a cocoon of comfort. Chocolate brown velvet, made up into simple panel curtains, hangs from matching rods. Leopard skin fabric upholsters a mushroom-shaped pouf.

Below: A paean to the artistry of the faux painter, this mantlepiece displays no fewer than eight difficult finishes. For those who would like to try their hand, schools that give classes in faux finishing methods have sprung up across the country.

Above: A pedimented marble mantlepiece and large modern oil painting purposely dwarf the small windows of this newly renovated home to give the living room a grander scale. The skylight also helps compensate for lack of square footage. A glass-topped coffee table makes the small conversation area seem more open and inviting.

Above: A mundane city apartment goes madcap with an infusion of color. Pastels, soft yellow for the front door and pale green for the sloping wall, are part of the background. Brilliant tones—fuchsia for the tufted sofa, periwinkle and yellow for the area rug—are very up front. The rest of the furnishings, as well as the fireplace facade, are sleek and black.

Opposite: The colors of the painted two-drawer side table served as an inspiration for the striking color combination used here. The mantlepiece and woodwork have been sponged buttercup yellow, the walls finished a deep teal blue. Bold hues like these tend to be most appealing when used in rooms with smallish dimensions.

Above: Embedded in stucco, broken pieces of curved terra-cotta roofing tile create this mantle's texture. Flawless skim-coated walls painted aubergine offer sleek contrast. The wrought-iron shelf and glass-topped table make a pleasing pairing in black and white. A checkerboard marble hearth provides a touch of playfulness.

Above: With open arms, an old chair of burnished leather and another upholstered with a Native American rug pattern welcome visitors to this pueblo-style home. Rough-hewn roof beams (called vigas), an unpainted wooden column, and a shuttered window suggest a rustic workman's hand here. Carved hanging shelves, a six-armed chandelier, and a diminutive, ornately framed oil over the fireplace lend a more worldly, Spanish feeling.

Above: A living room that must also serve as an entryway can pose furniture placement dilemmas. To make the room seem more open, it's best to place high-backed furnishings such as this rocker and wing chair against the long walls. Except in large rooms, avoid using area rugs, which tend to break up space. Here, a gleaming wood floor, recently refinished, adds a warm, cheerful glow as well as enlarges the room visually.

Chapter Three

Dining Areas

In most homes the dining room is the least utilized room in the house. Employed only for holiday meals, birthdays, and the occasional dinner party, it stands forlorn and forsaken, serving as a passageway to the eat-in kitchen, the broad, brown table a repository for the daily pile of mail. What a pity. What a waste. What can be done?

One tack is to make the dining room less formal and imposing, since this is the source of its disuse for most people. Like every other room, the dining room should reflect the way a family really lives. If cheeseburgers are served more often than chateaubriand, it seems silly to dine on antique porcelain plates beneath a crystal chandelier. Better to opt for another look—one more refined than fifties Formica but less opulent than Louis XIV. Decorate the room in a style everyone will feel comfortable dining in daily, at least for the evening meal.

Some homeowners, however, are loathe to relinquish the rarefied atmosphere of a formal dining room. What's more, they should not feel compelled to do so. In fact, a truly elegant dining space imbues any home with more than its share of beauty. The key is to use the dining room frequently, even if there's not time to take meals there. An unused room quickly achieves an aura of mustiness and stagnation.

There are many ways to make a formal dining room work for multiple purposes. One is to line a wall or walls with handsome shelves or bookcases filled with attractive hardbound volumes. Position a small comfy club chair or loveseat in a corner and add a lamp on a tiny table nearby. To any eye, the space has been transformed into a legitimate library even with the dining table and chairs still in place. A dining room might also do double duty as a home office or homework center with the help of a commodious sideboard or cabinet. Here, fax machine, laptop computer, and telephone, plus supplies and reference books, can all be stowed discreetly away until needed.

Whether they are formal or informal, all dining areas share the same basic requirements. Of these, the table is the largest element. From a budgeting standpoint the dining table offers a

Opposite: As fresh as fondant, this small dining area benefits from an array of pretty fabrics. Glints of gold can be found on the chairs, mirrors, sideboard, and chandelier. Crystal and silver provide additional sparkle.

distinct advantage over other necessary pieces of furniture. For a fraction of the cost of a new table, a stand-in or particleboard table of the appropriate size and shape can be covered with an attractive, floor-length tablecloth, and nobody will be the wiser.

Seating is the other element common to all dining rooms, and the seating style often sets the decorative scheme. By all means, choose chairs that are comfortable. Nothing is more satisfying than sitting in a seat that encourages lingering after dessert. If the chairs are used for everyday dining, it's practical to select those that have cushions that can be removed for regular cleaning. Also consider slipcovering dining room chairs for a change of pace as well as for holidays or other special occasions. "Many other pieces of furniture provide aid in serving or afford drawer space for table service and linens. These include sideboards, commodes, étagéres, and the like. Because tables and chairs are by nature short, it's desirable to have at least one tall storage piece, such as a breakfront, corner cupboard, or even a chest-on-chest, to help balance the room. Paintings and framed mirrors hung on the walls also help to give dining rooms a "lift." Mirrors, whether framed or mounted to the wall in vast expanses, also serve another purpose: to reflect candlelight and the sheen of polished silver. Chandeliers and fanciful overhead fixtures are used to better effect in the dining room than perhaps in any other setting.

In fact, every element used in a dining room should help create the desired mood as well as enhance the decor. In the dining room, it's the sense of contentment and relaxation that should hold sway.

Opposite: In less than expansive apartments, every effort should be made to make maximum use of existing space. With its built-in bookshelves, this dining room doubles beautifully as a place for reading and research once its nappery is put away. And, with recessed fixtures hooked up to a rheostat, lighting can go from low to librarylike.

Left: When an entry and a dining area converge, a sideboard can serve dual purposes. By day, this piece stores unsorted mail and dinnerware behind its quilted metal panels. During the evening, it functions as a serving station at formal and informal meals alike.

Below: An assortment of chairs, both rush- and cane-seated, and a lovingly worn rag rug are humble companions to the architecturally refined details found in this dining room. Equally varied accessories—including a mismatched collection of English dinnerware and a single silver candelabra—plus serious striped wallcovering help tie together the disparate elements.

Above: Whenever possible, display and store serving pieces close to the dining table. This way they'll be used almost daily rather than just gathering dust, forgotten at the bottom of a drawer or the back of a cupboard. These fortunate home-owners have a roomy hutch built into the original stone wall of their dining room. Its deep shelves hold their collection of vegetable-shaped pottery.

Above: Using red as a strong decorative accent in a space devoted to eating can enhance the appetite, according to various studies. But even a dieter can appreciate the richness this color provides. A dhurrie rug successfully defines the area's perimeter. To visually expand the square footage, choose a small round or oval table with removable leaves. Forgo these on a daily basis so that much of the rug underneath can show and the traffic ways remain open. Insert leaves when entertaining more than the usual number of guests.

Above: Even when the old table is not covered with its decorative cloth, this square dining room has eclectic charm. The chest-on-chest, a versatile piece of furniture too often confined to the bedroom, finds a welcome home here. In a dining room, a tall dresser like this one offers pleasing height and provides balance for the shorter pieces usually found in this space. It also offers deep-drawer storage for silver, large serving pieces, and table linens in a single convenient spot.

Above: An awkward, narrow room becomes a sunny spot for breakfast with the addition of a trestle table. When the dishes are cleared, its long expanse makes a great area for working on crafts or potting plants. Note that the ceiling has been painted a deep contrasting hue rather than traditional white. This makes the ceiling seem lower, which visually widens the dimensions of the room.

Above: Silver, crystal, and polished wood give this traditional dining room its appealing glow. Chintz curtains provide a soothing pattern. When the budget is tight, keep in mind that drapes needn't draw fully closed. All that is required is enough fabric to make the drapes attractively full when tied back. Behind the curtains hang not-so-sheer panels. These protect fabrics from fading and softly filter sunlight.

Below: These painted dining chairs, upholstered with a French provincial floral on the seat cushions and complementary pink plaid on the backs, imbue this dining area with its charming European feeling. An oil painting of a rose arrangement hangs above an unusual cabinet, while the trellis-patterned rug continues the garden theme. To keep the space from becoming overly feminine and flowery, the walls have been papered a deep green with a wide subtle stripe. Both the English dresser and the stout farm table lend a comfortable country air, as do pieces of majolica and pottery featuring barnyard friends.

Right: Glazed Delft-like tiles turn a plain-Jane chimneypiece into something truly special. In a casual dining setting such as this, hearths can be used for food preparation as long as appropriate implements and a fire extinguisher are near at hand. Here, the homeowners had the firebox fitted with an iron spit for roasting their favorite kinds of wild fowl.

FOCUSING ON FABRIC

To get the most value from an investment in fabric, it's essential to consider where the material will be used and its fiber content. There are three categories.

◆ *Naturals These tend to be comfortable and can be cleaned easily, but they attract dirt, may shrink or fade, and are often expensive.*

◆ *Synthetics Soil-resistant, these fabrics are tougher to clean, and can be scratchy, and some have a tendency to be shiny.*

◆ *Blends Part natural and part synthetic, blends can be your best bet. Be sure to check the feel, or "hand," of any fabric.*

Before purchasing fabrics or making selections for upholstered furniture and curtains, consider the following guides.

◆ *When shopping for upholstery fabric, remember that tweeds, prints, and plaids tend to age more gracefully than solids. Consider dense colorful prints if kids or pets (or both) are a problem. Jewel tones, neutrals, and mid-range hues are popular and likely will continue to be. These shades are also easier to maintain than very light or very dark colors.*

◆ *When selecting curtain fabric, gather one end and let a long piece of the material drape to the floor to see how it falls and what the pattern looks like when arranged in folds.*

◆ *Ask a salesperson to unroll any fabric bolt to see a quantity of the material. Look for any flaws including slubs, uneven grain, and inconsistency in color.*

◆ *Hold a piece of the fabric up to the light to get a look at the weave. The tighter the weave, the longer the fabric will wear.*

◆ *Rub pieces of the fabric together to be certain that there is no flaking.*

◆ *Stretch the fabric diagonally to be sure that individual threads do not separate or slip.*

◆ *Read the label thoroughly to find out about stain protection treatment, colorfastness, cleaning instructions, and content.*

Opposite: Before purchasing a dining table that will be used most often for entertaining, keep serving styles in mind. Several times each year, this host and hostess like to offer a large crowd an elegant buffet. To display multiple dishes and ease traffic flow, a long rectangular table best suits their purposes. The glass top eliminates the need for the protective pad and tablecloth that a wooden table might require. And when spills occur, this table wipes clean on the spot.

Right: Which came first, the dinnerware or the dining room? In this case, the color choices were nearly simultaneous. Most often, however, homeowners have already bought some good china before they begin remodeling or decorating this area. If those purchases still hold appeal, it's a sound idea to think about dish color and pattern before making any major decorating decision. Remember: pieces needn't match, but neither should they clash.

Above: Ocher yellow walls cast a warm glow in this diminutive, cozily crowded dining room. Its scaled-down furnishings of bird's-eye maple with ebonized accents strike a formal pose. Less serious touches include contrasting teal moldings and wicker chairs with plump, colorful pillows in a harlequinlike pattern.

Right: Industrial underpinnings make a monochromatic background for a bold, tropics-inspired oil pinting. Barrel chairs, glass table, and tiled floor offer cool, contemporary juxtaposition. When making a major purchase such as a painting, be sure that the piece will work well in at least one other room. Rotating art is a good way to make any space seem fresh without additional expense.

Left: Whether in the corner of a living room or a kitchen, banquette seating is a space-saving way to make a dining area. That's because the traffic area on one side of its table is eliminated. For a banquette, choose easy-to-clean materials like vinyl or stain-resistant fabrics. Also, make sure the banquette is amply padded and its seat height comfortable for the majority of family members and regular guests.

Opposite: More often than not, dining areas have multiple chairs with exposed legs. For this reason, it's best to avoid more of the same if the living area is adjacent. Instead, choose sofas and chairs with skirts, or low-slung pieces with upholstered legs as shown here.

Above: William Morris–style wallpaper infuses an otherwise lackluster breakfast area with color and character. A single curtain panel on a slender rod, gathered with a ribbon tie for a pretty look, provides a measure of privacy. A pair of antique chairs, a table, and a fringed tablecloth complete the nostalgic setting.

Below: The mullioned front of this new cabinet complements the divided-light window and French doors of this sunny dining area. It also offers easy access to everyday serving pieces. Underneath, a tambour door hides appliances and a tangle of electric cords. The old-fashioned pulls on the lower cabinet and its wooden counters contribute a country feeling. An age-burnished farm table beautifully handles the usual knocks from the large family that uses it for nearly every meal.

Above: Lovely antique furnishings in golden oak nestle perfectly between an awkward pair of windows. Dressed with pristine white roman blinds and café curtains hung on oversize rods and rings, the windows themselves recede into the background. Moldings and window frames need not, and in most cases should not, match the color of a room's furnishings. In this dining room, for example, more oak tones would be overkill.

Opposite:
Picasso's harlequin figure finds its way onto a cupboard door and tabletop in this small dining area. The nonartistic can rent or borrow an overhead projector to transfer favorite images onto desired surfaces and trace them. Inspiration, along with paint and sealer, should follow.

Above: Dining on the tiny porch of this summer cottage is delightfully laid-back. Table and chairs in contrasting hues send a message of spontaneity. They can also be folded, easily moved, and reset as the weather changes or the mood strikes for jigsaw puzzles or card games. The sisal checkerboard rug can be conveniently rolled up and stored at the end of the season.

Chapter Four

KITCHENS

*I*t's no fun hunting for the bain marie lost at the back of a crowded cabinet or having little counter space to set down a sizzling roasting pan. Whether one loves or hates to cook, the kitchen that best succeeds eases food preparation without sacrificing aesthetic appeal. Function comes first.

The question of the open floor plan plagues most homeowners remodeling kitchens today. The decision to open the space to the dining room, family room, or even the living room should be based on the wishes of the principal cook and the way the family prefers to interact and entertain. If the cook enjoys an audience for his or her culinary feats or just likes a chat while chopping up the vegetables for stew, the open plan makes a good choice—especially if the house's decorating style leans towards the informal. However, if the cook revels in some temporary solitude or thinks of the kitchen as a personal domain, the kitchen is best left contained (though not isolated), even if some square footage is available for the borrowing or a nearby room addition is planned.

There is some science to creating a kitchen that functions well. Many professionals who design kitchens begin by planning the work triangle. This consists of three imaginary lines between the sink, stove, and refrigerator. From a convenience standpoint, no line should be longer than two arm spans. And for comfort's sake, neither should these distances be so short as to constrict. Cast aside this ergonomic equation with caution. It has stood the test of time and all attendant trends.

Start with the sink. Position it, if possible, in front of or near a window. Since most of the time in the kitchen is usually spent here, this makes sense. So does siting the dishwasher near the sink. Whether a traditional range or a cooktop and wall oven combination is desired often determines the triangle's second segment. How this decision will affect the position, amount, and kind of storage should also be considered. It's ideal to plan storage space for cooking equipment and spices within arms' reach of the stove.

Opposite: Wainscot detailing and William Morris–style wall covering give this remodeled kitchen wing its turn-of-the-century charm. The cleverly designed counter, with its decorative back apron and winsome stenciling, creates a separate dining area screened from preparation mess. Tile covers the opposite wall, which is graced by a quaint upper cabinet and a lovely oval window. Below, a deep, wide sink has been fitted with a gooseneck faucet and old-fashioned porcelain fixtures for nostalgic charm.

At some point, too, the idea of the island or peninsula should be broached, space permitting. Extremely functional, the island or peninsula can act as room divider, snack counter, and extra food-prep surface as well as offer additional storage.

Of course, seldom does devising the layout incite enthusiasm when it comes to re-doing a kitchen. It's the decisions about style that make the blood run fast. Aside from strong architectural elements, such as a stone wall or a round window, cabinet choice generally communicates decorative direction. And purchasing or having new cabinets custom-made can be a costly undertaking. It is not, however, the only option. Outdated wooden cabinets can be restained, repainted, or sometimes refitted with new fronts. Painted tongue and groove, for example, can provide a custom look. Distinctive hardware, purchased on sale, also adds loads of style without too much expense.

Before making any decision on cabinetry, consider the traits of the person primarily responsible for keeping up the kitchen. Remember that open shelves and glass-fronted cabinets are for neatniks only. Those who hate to clean should purchase cabinets that meet the ceiling rather than those with soffit space. The choice eliminates a place for clutter to collect above.

Treatments for countertops, floor, and walls also have important decorative impact in the kitchen. And there are many beautiful choices, both natural and man-made, available today for these surfaces. However, since all three require regular cleaning, it's best to be practical. Keep in mind that those lovely tiled counters capture annoying debris in the grouting. Ceramic and terra-cotta tiles can become uncomfortable underfoot after lengthy periods. And papered backsplashes will begin to look soiled or worn quickly.

No matter whether its style is sleekly modern or quaintly country, a kitchen can be beautiful and clean, efficient and functional. In the end, careful planning makes things perfect.

Opposite: What one person calls clutter, another calls a collection. Before choosing a style for your kitchen, be certain of the camp that best suits. Here, a kitchen has been designed with a love of folk art in mind. The cabinets' raised panels, porcelain knobs, and painted trim suggest European influence, as does the soffit's frieze. A wine rack built into the lower cabinet is an efficient space-saver.

Left: Rough-hewn beams, butcher-block countertops, and wide-plank flooring help warm this all-white country kitchen. The large island can serve as a buffet when the family entertains informally in the adjoining dining area. Glass-front cabinets are particularly beautiful but could become the bane of those who are not particularly neat. If order doesn't come easily, choose glassfronts for a single display cabinet and keep everyday items behind paneled doors.

Above: Old wooden cabinets perk up with a colorful paint job, an inexpensive way to give a tired kitchen a terrific new look. Extra storage has been built and painted to house home-canned fruits and vegetables. The old farm table was found at a flea market, stripped of peeling paint, and refinished; the chairs are hand-me-downs.

Above: Now gleaming brightly in this small eclectic kitchen, a vintage stove and cabinets have been meticulously restored. Many companies specialize in this work, providing repairs as well as hard-to-find replacement parts. New tiling tops counters and covers the backsplash for extra sparkle. Wood beams and a posted center island offer countrified contrast.

Below: Like a retro icon, this still-working fridge is mounted on its own marble pedestal. Another commercial-grade refrigerator unit stands at the kitchen's other end, offering the required space to store food for large parties— or a large family! In between is a run of custom-crafted cabinetry and a large prep island.

FINDING OUT ABOUT VINYL FLOORING

Vinyl flooring is easy on the feet, durable, and a breeze to maintain by sweeping and occasionally mopping—perfect for the kitchen. There are three types available today.

◆ *Inlaid flooring Made of solid vinyl, this flooring fuses granules together to create color and pattern throughout the material. This is the most expensive and durable type of vinyl flooring.*

◆ *Rotovinyl The pattern of this flooring material consists of an image made by a photographic process, topped by a layer of clear vinyl. The thickness of the vinyl layer determines the durability and price of the flooring. The most expensive rotovinyl flooring has layers 25 mils thick. For a room that you plan to use regularly, don't consider rotovinyl flooring with layers less than 10 mils thick.*

◆ *Vinyl composition This flooring combines vinyl resins with filler materials. It is the most inexpensive and typically the least wear-resistant.*

Most vinyl flooring can be purchased either in sheets or as tiles. Sheet vinyl flooring tends to be more costly and should be installed by a professionals. Tile installation can be a do-it-yourself project (but beware that this might exclude your vinyl from the manufacturers warranty).

Vinyls are available in colors and textures of every description; some even mimic slate, wood, or ceramic tile.

Above: Black handles and pulls pepper the fronts of plain wooden cabinets in this suburban eat-in kitchen. A stylish wall oven, microwave, and cooktop in shiny black help to banish any possibility of blandness. Above the table, a pass-through to the dining room opens the entire area and exposes it to abundant sunshine. Flooring is low-maintenance vinyl tile in mostly gray with asymmetrical black accent pieces.

Opposite: In this small apartment, an old pantry cabinet has been preserved with its timeworn patina. The ceiling fixture and wall sconce are also elegantly burnished with age. New laminate cabinets and a ceramic tile backsplash provide contemporary counterpoints. On the floor, a classic checkerboard vinyl pattern straddles the eras. Moved from the living room, a butler's table performs as a self-service bar during parties.

Left: Funky yet simple and refreshing, this kitchen will appeal to those who love nostalgia and the recent past. Cabinets have been stripped bare, repainted their original color, and refitted with crystal knobs. The pink stove has also been refurbished, and grimy tiles have been professionaly cleaned. For a look like this to succeed, all the elements must be true to the period and restored to pristine condition.

Above: When undertaking a kitchen remodeling project, first decide which elements should be retained. An antique porcelain sink like this one is eminently practical and can even look pretty when old pipes are hidden behind a gathered skirt. The tile walls, too, have been left intact; a dark chintz makes them look pleasingly pastel rather than passé. Removing worn linoleum revealed solid wood floors, which have been sanded and stained. New to the room are a custom island as well as a matching run of cabinets and state-of-the-art appliances.

Left: This well-organized kitchen doesn't waste an inch of space. Cabinets meet the ceiling to maximize storage and eliminate a dust-catching soffit. Behind the mullioned cabinets all is in impeccable order. Sleek granite countertops border a downdraft gas cooktop and a deep, stockpot-welcoming sink.

Above: A "dishy" wallpaper plays up a display of plates in the beaded-board cabinets of this simple country kitchen. Papering behind the shelves of the mullioned doors would provide an even more finished look. Large squares of vinyl flooring create a bold checkerboard pattern. Laying tiles on a diagonal can give almost any space additional dash. Note the unmatched dining chairs and the comfy wingback.

Below: Beautiful Arts and Crafts–style cabinets are fitted with frosted glass panels etched with a simple motif of the nineteenth century. Wainscoting on the ceiling also recalls this earlier time. Terra-cotta floor tiles have been set with a border of glazed green accent pieces to simulate an area rug. The side-by-side freezer/refrigerator with polished stainless steel front quietly hums a tribute to present-day efficiencies.

Above: A refurbished fifties-style wall oven flanks a sleek, top-of-the-line refrigerator/freezer in this small funky kitchen; a range stands at the other end of the space. Original cabinets have been scraped to bare wood and repainted in two tones. Tiles set on the diagonal and finished with bull-nose trim replace the old laminate countertops. The whimsical blue marlin wallpaper border adds a tropical atmosphere.

Above: It's drawers galore for pots and pans and more in this contemporary kitchen. Honey blonde wood cabinets and matching narrowplank flooring warm this L-shaped space, while ebony-colored countertops and accents of stainless steel keep things crisp. Curved undercounter shelving and upper cabinet niches offer ample opportunities for display, and a cache of cookbooks is situated close at hand above the "homework" station.

Above: Sweeping countertops, soda fountain–style stools, and scintillating patterns show this kitchen to distinct advantage. For a twist on the basic checkerboard pattern, black and white tiles on the floor and on the dining peninsula are interspersed with pieces in fifties pastels. The refrigerator's front boasts a custom-striped panel that mimics the prep area's laminate inlay.

Below: Close quarters needn't make for clumsy design. This galley kitchen gained needed elbow room thanks to counters that are slightly narrower than standard. Custom cabinets reach the ceiling for more storage and house a microwave that might otherwise have gobbled up extra work space. Gleaming stainless steel is an easy-care choice for the sink, as is man-made surfacing material for the countertops. Wood flooring, with its natural "give," is more comfortable than ceramic tile underfoot.

Right: Wood counters and sea-foam-colored glass panels soften the professional demeanor of this gourmet cook's kitchen, furbished with stainless steel appliances and a large cooktop vent. The old-fashioned honeycomb-style tile floor and office stool are both practical and decorative. French doors proffer fresh air and light, and served as inspiration for the cabinets' design.

Chapter Five

FAMILY ROOMS AND LIBRARIES

Opposite: Beautifully burnished pine paneling casts a mellow glow in this family room. Its rustic feeling is enhanced by the wide chair rail and horizontal planking used as wainscoting as well as the distressed coffee table. Bovine prints and porcelains bolster the pastoral theme. Other elements—including the deep floral upholstery fabric with brush and bullion fringes and the leopard-patterned carpet and pillow—purposely raise the level of sophistication.

The television set, perhaps more than any other invention, is responsible for changing the interior of the modern home. It, in fact, gave rise to a brand-new room—the family room—and today no right-minded builder would construct a home without one. Not surprisingly, although most members of the typical clan remain somewhat confused about the function of the living room, even the two-year-old knows with certainty that the family room is for TV watching. Of course, other activities also take place here, but watching television is the room's mainstay. Most homeowners unhesitatingly plan the space around this latter-day hearth. Here in the family room they even feel free from the need to hide "the box."

When the principal function and the focal point of a room are one and the same, it would seem a cinch to arrange the furniture. However, a circle of chairs around the tube lacks appeal even to the untrained eye. It would seem that creating a more balanced arrangement also means disadvantaged viewing for some. There are, however, ways to alleviate this problem. The first is to be sure to include several comfortable but easily moved chairs as well as an ottoman or two in the seating arrangement. Another option is to use more club chairs or other large upholstered chairs, but to purchase these with swivel mounts hidden by their skirts.

Because it is the room used most frequently, the family room poses another problem: wear and tear. Upholstery fabric and rugs are at particularly high risk. Although the family room is usually more casual in feeling than the living room, a stiff synthetic blend is not necessarily the only fabric suitable for this space. Do, however, choose materials that are tightly woven, medium to dark in hue, preferably patterned, and stain-resistant. Avoid carpeting, which will eventually show soil and wear in front of the viewing area while appearing absolutely pristine around the room's perimeter.

Before there were family rooms in homes, there were libraries. It was here rather than the parlor that the family would settle in to read and perhaps converse. The library continues to function in this way today, but make no mistake: a room with books on shelves is not necessarily a library. By visual definition, a library must display devotion to learning, and no single element expresses this pursuit more clearly than the bookcase.

There are many styles to consider. However, a built-in bookcase, particularly one that appears as part of a room's architecture, makes the strongest statement. When having these designed and constructed, pay particular attention to the cornices, pilasters, and bases. These should mimic the style of the molding, baseboards, or other details in the room. The length of each bay of shelves can also echo the width of the door or window if these exist on the opposite wall.

Lighting, of course, is exceedingly important in the library. A good reading lamp is a must. Floor lamps with rheostats that allow for infinitesimal adjustments are particularly welcome here. Seating is the library's other essential element. A comfortable upholstered chair and a footrest are absolutely required. Refrain, however, from selecting a chair that's too soft. Instead, look for one with good back support. Otherwise reading sessions will inevitably turn into siestas.

Opposite: On rainy days this airy family room, converted from an enclosed porch, makes a cozy gathering place. The slipcovered club chair is the perfect spot for a daughter reading a Nancy Drew mystery. The timeworn wicker settee welcomes Mom for needlepoint sessions. Its bowed back is dressed up with an embroidered tea cloth; a faded thirties-style kitchen cloth camouflages the plain game table. Using "heirloom" fabrics such as these ties disparate furnishings together in a simple, charming way. In the true spirit of a family room, artwork of children is mixed with favorite prints to decorate walls.

Left: Perennially cozy, this Victorian library is true to period, with its dark woodwork and rich wallpaper in a complex pattern. An authentic, eclectic mix of furnishings displays many influences, including baroque, rococo, and neoclassical. An Oriental throw and pillows make the room's daybed an even more tempting spot to relax with a leather-bound volume pulled from the exuberantly carved corner bookcase.

Above: The coffee table, made from an old battered door, immediately sends "put your feet up" signals in this Southwestern-style family room. Mission furniture and a camelback sofa upholstered in Native American blanket fabric underscore the relaxed scheme, and rugged ceiling beams serve to reinforce it. Folk art pieces and Native American pottery are comfortably at home in this informal room. Corniced bookcases have been custom-built and create a nestling spot for a love seat.

Below: Here, a Southwestern-style family room plays a pronounced "home on the range" theme. Cowboy boot bookends and a bucking bronco bronze decorate the rough-hewn mantelpiece; horses emblazon a firescreen below. Checkered game boards provide a strong graphic element as well as a source of quiet entertainment.

Above: Using naive and handcrafted accessories keeps this family room from appearing overly formal despite its host of traditional furnishings. Tin cherub silhouettes, a folk art oil painting, and a columned birdhouse are foils for the marble-topped sideboard and elegant candlesticks in this carefully arranged vignette.

Opposite: Family rooms can be great places to display unusual collections. Pieces that might appear too prosaic or casual in the living room are more apropos here. This homeowner chose a Chinese red in a glossy eggshell finish to serve as a vibrant and unifying background for her collection of antique hooked rugs and stuffed dolls. Shutters and trim are also painted red to more readily disappear and not compete with the collectibles. Bold splashes of cobalt in the form of hanging china plates break up the wash of color without destroying the scheme. Piles of mismatched pillows on a comfy couch finish this inviting corner.

Above: A fifties fanatic turned a guest room into a funky family room using favorite pieces from the past. The lamp, sofa, and easy chair were all found at secondhand furniture stores. An eccentric rug featuring a map of the United States is laid on the diagonal, giving the square room a new angle; the couch follows the line dictated by the rug. The bracketed memorabilia shelves, filled with hundreds of kitschy curios, are homemade. Their curved ends mimic the lines of the mirrored dressing table that once would have been found only in a bedroom.

Above: Two bays of bookshelves flank a simple stone mantel in this family room accessorized with a subtle maritime theme. Tactile white linen covers a pair of upholstered chairs as well as the sofa. The tomes themselves provide needed splashes of color. Wooden furnishings, all with underlying golden tones, complement the sunny walls.

Below: Despite its elaborate crown moldings and ceiling treatment, restraint characterizes this beautiful library. A monochromatic color scheme in varying shades of beige brings its unusual collection of furnishings to the forefront. The room is, in fact, a "study" in contradictions. Compare the pair of upholstered chairs: although they share the same leg style and fabric, each has been dressed differently. One has been turned out tailored and trim; the other is garbed in a flirty box-pleated skirt. Note, too, how the pair of lithe end tables contrasts with the bun-footed coffee table.

Above: Home theater becomes the hearth in this contemporary family room. Pieces of laminate function as artwork as well as a frame for the in-wall media unit. A lamp constructed of wire and white fabric is both sculpture and light source. An outspoken "comics" fabric tops the occasional table. Chair and sofa reply in witty hues.

Left: In this somewhat formal family room, furry fringe on moiré-patterned, slipcovered furnishings is an element of fun. The valance has been treated to some unusual swirling passementerie. A curtain-lined armoire contains the television and breakfast fixings.

Opposite: When its door is closed, a cleverly constructed cabinet for the television and stereo mimics the entry to this family room. The hand of a talented carpenter is apparent throughout the space—from moldings to mantelpiece and from windowsills to baseboards.

Above: The round table, piled with a mountain of books, never looked better than in this spacious high-ceilinged study. Painted a deep sienna, the walls marry well with the lovingly restored and stained pilasters, moldings, and window frames. Tiers of wooden shutters are a handsome and practical way to control the amount of sunlight entering the room and look less fussy than curtains. Because they share similar wood tones, the assorted eclectic furnishings work comfortably as companions.

Above: Like most well-thought-out family rooms, this one encourages many functions. The comfy couch and chairs beckon adults and children to relax and watch television together. The space also serves as an informal dining room as well as a cocktail area when there's crowd overflow from the patio beyond. Multiple fabric patterns in floral chintz, stripes, and geometrics contribute a cottagelike air as does the old workbench standing in as the coffee table. Underfoot, a rag rug and small antique carpet extend the layered look. A framed "passed down" quilt completes the picture.

UNDERSTANDING PAINT

Before buying paints, it's wise to know their composition and how they will stand up to use. Keep in mind that terms like "flat," "semi-gloss," "eggshell," and "satin" indicate how a paint reflects light—not its durability.

◆*Oil-based paints Sometimes called alkyds when a synthetic resin is used instead of natural oils, these paints are durable and hold up to repeated scrubbings. An oil-based paint is an excellent choice for heavy traffic areas: it is especially good for areas that will be "handled," such as railings and windowsills. Oil-based paints resist moisture better than most water-based paints, so select them as well for bathrooms, kitchens, and other areas where water and high humidity are present.*

Oil-based paints take longer to dry than water-based formulas. Also, oil paints will reveal imperfections, so nicks and dents in woodwork should be filled before you paint.

◆*Water-based paints These are easier to work with, give off less fumes during application, and are typically less expensive than oil-based paints. Most are made with latex and dry quickly.*

Water-based paints are a good choice for bedrooms, the living room, the dining room, and other areas that don't get a lot of wear and tear.

Chapter Six

BEDROOMS

Because the bedroom is the most private room in the house, it offers that very rare opportunity: to please only oneself. In every other space, design concessions must frequently be made to meet the needs of guests and family members, but in the bedroom, individual—even idiosyncratic—preferences may reign supreme. Here is the perfect space to display the odd assortment of personal treasures or indulge in whimsical styles. Baring the soul, decoratively speaking, will make the room more intimate, a mood to which all bedrooms should aspire.

Granted, some people feel most comfortable in simple, spartan surroundings, and these include bedrooms. A pared-down look needn't be pleasureless, however. Style considerations aside, all bedrooms should boast at the very least a comfortable mattress, lovely, fresh linens, a good reading light, a sturdy chair, and something beautiful to look at—be it a mountain view or a bowl of succulent grapes.

More often than not, however, people do enjoy luxurious trappings in their bedrooms. To want for nothing enhances a sense of refuge. A soft throw for an impromptu nap, a bedside water carafe of sparkling crystal, notepaper and pencils in a handsome box—these are accoutrements easily acquired and deeply cherished, for the bedroom is generally used for more than sleeping. Reading, needlepointing, crossword puzzling, television watching, and other relaxing pursuits all take place here. It's best to preserve the bedroom as a sanctuary and push forward elsewhere on tedious tasks such as paying bills or completing office work. In truth, waking up to a desk piled high with papers can have a negative effect on the whole day.

Those who share a bedroom should keep in mind their partner's preferences when decorating the bedroom. Some men are made uneasy by what they consider an overly feminine scheme. Not to worry—there are plenty of ways to compromise. For example, when choosing a floral chintz, look for one in which vines are nearly as dominant as the blossoms, and see if this doesn't appease him. Or, rather than choosing a pale pink paint for the walls, select some-

Opposite: This four-poster might be wider than the space between the windows, but that's not necessarily a problem. Simple panels that match the color of the cutwork canopy fall behind each of the headboard's posts, creating the effect of a bona fide bed hanging. To avoid overpowering the space, the scale of the other furnishings and pictures in the room is diminutive.

thing from the same spectrum with an underlying earthy tone. Forgo frills and ruffles on the bedding, opting instead for a more tailored look. These few accommodations can go a long way toward both marital and decorative harmony.

Furnishings generally provoke less dissent than color and fabric in shared bedrooms. The bed, of course, is the largest and most important piece to consider because it is the room's focal point. Beds in four-poster, canopy, platform, and padded headboard styles are perennially popular. What's essential, though, is that the bed not overpower the room or seem silly or pretentious. Scale and architectural elements make the best guides in this instance.

Unlike the master bedroom, the guest room should be created solely with others' needs in mind. Certainly it should be as comfortable as the master suite. Reposeful mattress, both synthetic and down pillows, lined curtains to keep out the sun, fluffy towels, and fragrant linens are musts. If possible, a guest room should also contain a table, a desk, or another surface on which to write. This also makes a good spot for a plate of fruit, a bottle of water, stationery, and a few books and magazines. For a truly marvelous guest room, provide all the comforts of home plus the same degree of privacy. After all, sharing simple pleasures with people you care for is what bedrooms are all about.

Opposite: Beaded-board walls would hardly seem the appropriate backdrop for an empire-style bed, but somehow this attic room works. The slate blue used for the wall repeats on the striped slipper chair and the tufted, turned-leg chair upholstered with ticking. The soleil mirror reflects the gilding of the bedposts. Punctuation points of black appear in the wrought-iron floor lamp, the glass-topped table, and the framed prints on the pale wood floor.

Left: To make this small dormer room seem larger, its diamond-patterned wall covering runs across the ceiling, too. Coordinating border paper has been used at chair-rail height to help anchor the room; striped, coordinated wall covering used below breaks up the monotony. A richly colored roman shade offers complete darkness for the late riser; the paper shade provides privacy plus opaque light for the daydreamer. The dresser, with its crackled finish, is a proper resting place for black-eyed Susans and a collection of river stones.

Above: With some careful thought, even a boxy apartment bedroom can be transformed into a beckoning retreat. A four-poster might seem an unusual choice for such a small area, but because the bed is painted white and its lines are so simple, it appears to take up less space. Its height also draws the eye upward, enhancing the room's proportions. Using a brilliant shade for the bedspread is a disarming and, in fact, charming idea here. The heirloom chest topped with an eyelet runner helps to personalize the room; accessories like the butterfly tray, soft pastels, and potted plants reveal a love of nature.

Right: A tented top sets a pie-in-the-sky tone in this small master bedroom. Vertical striping keeps the ceiling from feeling too low, while the flaglike border helps hide the tenting structure and adds a festive note. Although many other patterns, including a plaid and two other prints, are used here, their muted colors keep the mood mellow and masculine. Wooden blinds and a roman shade are wisely simple treatments for the nondescript window. A small bamboo screen is ideal for concealing a radiator, stacks of boxes, or even exercise equipment, and provides a pleasing deviation from the square lines of the room.

Left: All is sumptuous serenity in this sophisticated master bedroom with a monochromatic color scheme. Heavy, beige cotton tumbles in flowing pleats from a box-pleated tester, a treatment that is echoed at the tall window. The same fabric upholsters roll-armed chairs. Only the antique Oriental rug and the banding on the large Japanese cabinet, which stows a television and stereo, display decorative patterning.

Above: Frequently the sexes battle over the decoration of the bedroom. A perfect melding of masculine and feminine desires has been achieved here, due to creative and contrasting use of color and texture. The deep-hued walls and paisley throw satisfy his longing for strong color and luxurious pattern; white bedspread and pillows quell her pining for the pristine. The sisal rug appeases his penchant for the practical; frothy curtains with rosette valance and a needlepoint rug appeal to her love of flowers.

Below: This ornate brass bedstead could have looked hopelessly heavy had it been fitted with the dark and opulent coverings of its period. Instead, beautiful, soft-washed linen makes up the bedspread, and featherlight chiffon with a voluminous underskirt billows as the dust ruffle. Because neither privacy nor early morning light are issues, chiffon with rope tiebacks also hangs at the windows. Wide-plank floorboards are left noticeably bare to underscore the room's overall simplicity.

Above: This room is a study in creativity and adaptability—none of the furnishings are used as originally intended, but they suit their new stations well, acting in concert to create a fantastical yet comfortable retreat. A French-style sofa upholstered in creamy linen finds new life as a headboard. Poles suspended from the ceiling support a length of sheer cotton to form a canopy. Photographer's lights used as reading lamps are a tongue-in-cheek touch. A varnished tree stump serves as a bedside table, fostering a connection between indoors and out.

Below: Like those of many southern porches, the ceiling of this attic dormer room is painted sky blue. Rafters and the beaded board below are treated to a bright white enamel. Neoclassical elements such as the columned pedestal, the plaster bust, and the Greek key pattern on the duvet cover comfortably coexist with quirky wooden and upholstered chairs and a pair of stools.

Above: A bed, sitting area, and long, glass-topped storage counter make this attic room a real retreat. In any guest room, it's a good idea to create an area where a visitor can spread out a few papers or at least write a letter. There should also be a place to sit and read. More often than not, guests appreciate function as much as decorative flourishes.

Above: There's nothing fancy about the furnishings in this serene space. In fact, the bedside table and iron headboard were both found at flea markets. Each, however, has been carefully restored. The table's apron and the bed's headboard share undulating lines that echo each other. With newly painted walls, crisp white roman shades, and freshly picked roses in a creamware pitcher, it's a room that is inviting in its simplicity.

Below: Akin to a ship's cabin, this bedroom squanders nary a square inch. Snuggled between two doors and positioned underneath a porthole window, the platform bed hides a wide, deep drawer in its custom base. In lieu of bedside tables, narrow bookcases are set into the wall on either side of the niche to house books, an alarm clock, and other essentials. The mattress support has been stained a deep teak color to match the floor. Recessed lighting on dimmer switches permits changing peach-colored walls from pale to pronounced depending on intensity.

Opposite: Colors and fabrics from the sixties meet up with materials from the nineties. Eye-popping yellow and orange pillows and a sable-colored, crushed velvet coverlet conjure up pads from an earlier era. But the brushed aluminum armoire and stained and polished wooden floor are stylistic elements of the moment. Artwork resting on the headboard continues the wild color scheme.

Above: Devoted readers chose this architecturally inspired headboard to keep their books from cluttering up the bedroom. Like a mantelpiece in a living room, its lines enhance this space's beautifully restored moldings and trim. Affixed to the bed, a pair of brass swing-arm lamps fitted with rheostats can be infinitely adjusted for position and degree of illumination. The dressing table echoes the design of the bed; square columns on either side of the oval mirror are sedate yet whimsical. An all-white color scheme allows the strong, architectural furniture to take center stage.

Opposite: A dressing table can take up surprisingly little space, as this narrow room proves. Made from particleboard cut into a classic serpentine shape, this example is topped with a mirror and dressed in a skirt with a triple pencil-pleated heading. The Chinese garden seat used as a small table for the tufted slipper chair continues the floral scheme. Lace panels hung from a wall-mounted pole fall on either side. So as not to over-do, windows are fitted with plain shutters rather than draped with fabric, and architectural drawings provide a welcome respite from feminine frills.

SELECTING THE RIGHT CARPETING

It's important to understand carpeting before making a costly purchase that is expected to last for years. Carpet construction, the way the yarn is tufted or set into a backing, and its content all contribute to the carpet's texture, durability, and appearance.

CONSTRUCTION

◆ *Cut pile* *Loops are cut, leaving yarn tufts at the surface. This is one of the most popular carpeting types. Its durability is determined by the fiber used, the density of the tufts, and the degree of twist in the yarn.*

◆ *Level-loop pile* *Loops of equal height make up the surface. This carpeting is highly durable so it is ideal for heavy traffic areas, such as family rooms. Many of the popular Berbers are level-loop pile.*

◆ *Multilevel-loop pile* *Pattern effects are created with two or three different loop heights. This carpeting also features excellent durability.*

◆ *Cut-and-loop pile* *This combination of yarn tufts and loops produces texture on the surface and includes sculptured styles.*

CONTENT

There are five basic types of carpet pile fibers.

◆ *Nylon* *Two-thirds of all American-made pile fibers are nylon. It is wear-resistant, withstands the weight and movement of furniture, and provides vivid color. It also resists stains and is recommended for high-traffic areas.*

◆ *Olefin (polypropylene)* *This fiber is easily cleaned and notably colorfast; it is low-static and can withstand indoor/outdoor applications thanks to moisture and mildew resistance.*

◆ *Polyester* *Noted for its softness when used in thick cut-pile carpets, polyester has excellent color clarity, is easy to clean, and resists water-soluble stains.*

◆ *Acrylic* *Most similar to wool without the expense, acrylic is low-static and mildew-resistant. It is frequently used in level-loop constructions.*

◆ *Wool* *Noted for luxury and performance, wool is soft, has bulk, and comes in many colors. It is generally more expensive than synthetics.*

TERMS

◆ *Density* *This refers to the amount of yarn in the carpet and the closeness of the tufts; dense piles offer thicker, lusher carpets.*

◆ *Twist* *This describes the winding of the yarn around itself; the tighter and better defined the twist, the higher the durability.*

Below: When the budget is particularly tight, expense can be spared by creatively recycling pieces of forlorn furniture. Here, in a country house, a cabinet file goes undercover with carefully applied vinyl-coated paper. Its bold stripe stands up to the large floral used for the Austrian blind and matching wall covering. The deep green selected for the side chair was drawn from the pattern's well-rendered foliage. Roses overflowing from pottery vases and a beveled mirror with a hand-painted frame continue the floral theme without seeming forced.

Above: Dare to be bold in rooms not used every day. Replete with stripes, this dormer room is a place for both work and restful retreat. A table fitted with a slipcover holds a personal computer and cleverly hides supplies beneath. The upholstered daybed creates a haven for relaxing with a good book and doubles as an extra bed for guests.

Above: A well-worn, reproduction serpentine-front dresser benefits from a bit of decoupage in the nostalgic summerhouse bedroom of a devoted handicrafter. Panels covered with machine-embroidered, tea-stained cloth and set into the moldings are a pretty way to cover imperfections in the walls, and are far less expensive than replastering. Grosgrain ribbons and brass tacks have been ingeniously worked into a bulletin board; fringe, clipped from an old tablecloth found at a flea market, makes a festoon for the iron headboard. Rich details like the amber glass glinting in the window and the diminutive Victorian-style lamp add a polished look.

Left: In a guest room, a pair of mahogany four-posters have been dressed with simple cotton draping in an open-square pattern. Cutwork throw pillows complement the beds' airy design. Pushing them together makes the beds appear as a single unit and creates space for a small dresser. To help balance the height of the beds, the window has been draped with flowing pleated panels affixed to a pole mounted at the ceiling. The rod is covered with an elegantly ruched matching fabric. Stacks of books and a multitude of family photographs atop a graceful table are personal touches that put guests at ease.

Right: Collectibles shouldn't be hidden away behind glass doors. Even unusual objects can be used or displayed in inventive ways. A decorative verge board that once graced the eave above the front door of a Gothic Revival house now stands in as a charming headboard. An antique birdhouse is another favorite piece from this homeowner's cache of folk art. The crisp blue and white bedcoverings and flawless wall paint are necessary backdrops to timeworn objects.

Above: Luxurious fabrics in a multiplicity of textures make this bedroom particularly sensual. Linen, cotton matelassé, fine merino wool, and silk damask have been used in appetizing shades of creme, café au lait, and nutmeg. A cutwork tablecloth has been used as a bed hanging. Old wooden blinds, cleaned and refurbished with new taping, filter light and temper the urban view. To maximize space in this tiny room, a black lacquer tray set atop the radiator cover serves as a bedside table.

Above: When arranging a room, it's not easy to overcome awkwardly placed windows and doors. This is particularly true in a master bedroom, where a queen-size mattress limits options. Here, only one wall was wide enough for the bed, but its placement drew attention to unattractive corner windows. A round bedside table skirted with a crazy quilt softens their brash angularity, and plain roman blinds also help to downplay them. Note, too, that the blinds are hung well above the windows' frames to make the ceiling seem higher. Painting the lower portion of the wall a deeper tone accomplishes the same. The lighter color painted above draws the eyes upward.

Above: This pared-down bedroom celebrates the spirit of the Southwest. Its beautiful, burnished wood floor and wide, knotty pine baseboards help set the tone. The stucco walls have been left noticeably bare, save for one small, naive oil painting. Unbleached muslin panels cascade from a pair of tall casement windows that create a sun-filled niche for the turned-post bed. Though colors are predominantly neutral, folded Indian blankets and a bedspread in a saturated blue supply appealing accents. An antique, leather-topped stool used as a nightstand and a wicker storage trunk are the only other furnishings required.

Opposite: When the owners decided to make their bedroom as rustic in feeling as the rest of their remodeled home, they decided to have wide-paneled wainscoting installed. In a moment of inspiration, they topped it with extra-wide molding. This created a shelf to display pieces from a collection of Americana as well as prints and photographs. A colorful Native American blanket brightens the otherwise neutral palette.

Above: Expansive walls tinted the faintest shade of blue and yards of fabric in a small dotted pattern prevent the florals and feminine touches in this master bedroom from appearing overly frilly. In addition, the cabbage rose print on a deep-hued background balances the paler, more delicate tones of cream and rose, adding a pleasing depth to the picture. The absence of a footboard on the bed allows the eye to travel unimpeded to the spectacular view from the open French doors.

Above: Silk. Chiffon. Satin. Nothing could make a room feel more luxurious than a bed dressed in these fabrics. The ruffled and lace-edged hangings float down and around the lacquer headboard inlaid with mother-of-pearl. The draping also draws attention to the molding and border at the ceiling. A painted lacquer screen provides weight and balance as well as additional romance. Apricot-yellow walls are treated to gilt floral bouquets, which are repeated in the gilt-framed prints. An unusual child's chair is shaped like a scallop shell.

Above: Despite the Middle Eastern pattern of its bedclothes, the patois of this room is essentially northern European. The semicircular crown canopy attached to the wall and the arched fabric headboard have a decidedly French accent. The console table used as a desk and the damask-covered side chairs, however, express an English sensibility. The predominant use of blue for fabrics and the porcelain lamps and plates make the design statement coherent.

Chapter Seven

BATHROOMS

*D*uring the last two decades, the bathroom has undergone a major transformation. Once a strictly utilitarian space, today many new and remodeled bathrooms resemble mini spas, luxuriously sheathed in marble and complete with whirlpools, skylights, shower enclosures for two, bidets, and even exercise bicycles. Unfortunately, this modern take on the Roman bath often requires lots of square footage as well as Herculean amounts of money.

The good news is that without diving too deep into the savings account, nearly any bath can be transformed into a sybaritic retreat. To avoid unnecessary expense, try to work with the positive points that the existing bathroom possesses. At first, these might not be obvious, but a contractor or designer should be able to help. Good plumbing lines are one such example. Retaining the position of the waste line and stack can save money. If, however, an awkward layout is one of the reasons for the remodeling, it's perhaps best to plunge ahead and reposition the fixtures.

The sink is usually best situated near a window to take advantage of natural light for shaving or for makeup application. Provided some precautions have been taken for privacy, the bathtub also can be placed to advantage near a window. Many people like to have the toilet installed in a separate compartment so that more than one person can use the bathroom at a time. This is a particularly good idea for baths shared by the entire family. If this is not possible, the toilet is best placed out of the sight line of the door. In small bathrooms, it's a good idea to rehang doors so that they swing out rather than in. Be sure, though, that this doesn't create problems in the adjacent room or hallway.

Once the preliminary plan is on paper, the time has come to select the fixtures. Pedestal and wall-hung sinks are available from manufacturers in any number of styles. Loss of hideaway storage is a downside of these models. Even the smallest under-sink cabinet can hold lots of necessities, including cleaning supplies, linens, and personal care items. Tubs, whether clawfooted porcelain, sleek stainless steel, or Japanese-style stone, add splash to any bath. Be sure

Opposite: With doors leading both to the garden and the pool, this beautiful all-white bath is dappled by day with warm sunlight so it never appears unappealingly cold. Wonderful natural views temper its apparent formality. At night, recessed lighting helps focuses attention on the subtle ceramic trim and tile work as well as the classically columned sink.

to think carefully before deciding on a very large tub or whirlpool. Consider how often it will be used, the space it will require, and whether the floor will need additional support.

Set up separately from the tub, a shower stall makes a truly marvelous addition. Given the appropriate layout, even the smallest bathroom can generally accommodate one. Unfortunately, many of the stock shower enclosures now available are not as attractive as they might be. If nothing on the market appeals, perhaps a contractor or bath designer can come up with an innovative idea. Just make sure the solution is watertight!

When it comes to creating a bathroom's decor, surface treatments and cabinetry can be as important as the fixtures. Because humidity can take its toll even in well-ventilated baths, tough, impermeable surfaces are safe bets. Paint used in the bathroom, whether on walls, floor, or woodwork, should be durable and made to withstand heat and dampness. Hang only washable or scrubbable wall covering and be sure to use a primer that contains mold and mildew retardants.

Whether large or small, every bathroom needs a mirror. A mirrored medicine cabinet provides storage, but many are unattractive. A stylish, framed mirror can be employed instead and might even be hinged from behind to take advantage of existing recessed space. Expanses of mirror can also be used to make a room appear larger. Before giving the glazier the go-ahead, however, think about the images, naked and otherwise, the mirror will reflect.

Lastly, to enhance its havenlike feeling, a bath must have artwork or decorative accessories that reflect the tastes and interests of those who use it. The sentimental, silly, or surreal things that have no place in a home's public rooms might be perfect for the bath. Surrounding oneself with images and objects that please is part of the renewal process, an integral function of the well-designed bath.

Opposite: Like sunken treasure, this bath promises a wealth of pleasure. As the jets of the whirlpool massage sore muscles, a soft breeze blows through the double doors leading to the garden. A bamboo armchair sits near the entrance in the sun. Here, the towel-clad can warm themselves and quietly contemplate the purity of this room and the beauty of its hand-cast terra-cotta pavers.

Left: Part dressing room, part bathroom, and completely charming, this space is large enough to accommodate a dresser and a large gilt mirror. Antique silver-topped crystal jars and bottles and a sterling brush set add to the sense of refinement. Dark floral wall covering is overtly nostalgic. The tattersall fabric shower curtain in complementary hues represents a tailored, more modern turn.

Left: Take one marble-topped Victorian dressing table. Add a bold striped floral wall covering that flatters its warm hues. Mix in a contemporary metal chair with a striped cushion. Finish with an assortment of accessories from a variety of periods. The result? An eclectic dressing room that's wonderfully witty and surprisingly cozy.

Above: Stone pillars and walls are warmed in this Western-style home by the glowing wood paneling and furnishings found in nearly every room. This bathroom is no exception. Its custom-made cabinet with double doors and drawers has a beautiful ruddy color. The brass gooseneck faucet adds a gleam of its own. Opposite, the shower has been hung with a curtain made from fabric patterned after a Native American blanket.

Above: A lush Victorian wall covering, some grouting and tile repairs, plus sets of exquisite hand towels transformed this old-fashioned bath. Rather than completely redoing such spaces, many homeowners who like this look decide to make other minor fixes such as having stained or worn tubs and sinks reglazed by a professional using a new bonding method. The results can be extremely satisfactory.

Opposite: A talented painter ragged the walls of this bathroom to look like smooth stone. The artist also turned his brush to the tub surround, transforming wood into faux marble. A Victorian mirrored whatnot, which at one time had been attached to either a console table or a dresser, is now an "over the top" accessory. It hangs from the room's longest wall, successfully breaking up this expanse.

Right: This bathroom's basin, poised on a length of marble, looks delightful rather than dated. Juxtaposed with the opulent crystal chandelier, its plainness is even more pleasing. Original honeycomb tile on the wall is left as it was. Mirrors from a bus flank the windows and are just for fun.

Below: Even though this bathroom has been completely remodeled, it has a turn-of-the century temperament. The new wall covering copied from an old design has a "time-mellowed" ground. The curved, routed edges of the vanity resemble the profile of the marble tops used for Victorian chests of drawers. A collection of antique sterling silver figured boxes lines the counter's narrow length.

Above: So discreet. A carved and painted chair in the style of Louis XV has a hinged seat. Caning covers both the tank and bowl. The curtains in this bathroom are, by contrast, unassuming and made of unlined cotton with a rod-pocket heading. French-style wall covering is simply sweet.

Above: More than any other material, tile sends a strong message in the bath. Keep in mind, however, that because it can be expensive to replace, this statement is often enduring. Available in myriad colors and patterns, ceramics and various trims and moldings can be used for floors, ceilings, counters, and tub and mirror surrounds. Here, teal-colored rectangles have been set in staggered horizontal rows reminiscent of brickwork in the tub's enclosure. Accent pieces with a loosely twisted rope pattern break up this field. Leaf-patterned accents edge the large counter-flush mirror.

Above left: With its extensive use of marble and wood, this bathroom pays homage to nature and the tranquility that its materials, when crafted with care, can provide. This contemporary take on the Japanese soaking tub is just one element in a space where the art of relaxation has been elevated to a higher level.

Above right: The sink is the centerpiece of the powder room in this architecturally adventurous home. An octagonal wall-mounted vanity holds a stainless steel basin with a pebbled finish. A beveled mirror cut at an acute angle offers another lesson in geometry. The gooseneck faucet and winged fixtures are other flights of fancy.

Opposite: Bathing outdoors is an instinctual desire, yet one difficult to satisfy for most people. These fortunate homeowners found a way to assuage it to great effect. By constructing a wall of glass that fronts a small walled garden, they are free to enjoy the fresh air, the golden sunlight, and the earthy fragrance of the varietal plantings while also enjoying a sensuous soak.

Above: In the small bathroom of this country cottage, walls and waincoating were simply repainted, happily delaying the prospect of a complete remodeling. A fresh coat of bright white makes old fixtures disappear into the background, and a collection of old glass apothecary bottles provides the needed dose of jewellike color.

Below: All-white bathrooms needn't look boring. An assortment of the right accessories can make even an older bath that has seen better days an attention getter. Here, antique silver cups make useful repositories for a collection of ivory combs. Both sit on an old tray-topped iron stand that might have held plants on a porch or in a conservatory. Its legs are nearly as elegant as the slender stems of the fresh orchid atop the pedestal sink.

Above: Rather than replacing a serviceable tub and sink, an old-fashioned bathroom gets a face lift with the help of some heavy cotton fabrics in beige and white. With its heading made of braided welting, a windowpane check skirts the basin, creating needed storage and hiding unsightly pipes. Jumbo welting, also braided, ties back the double-faced shower curtain attached to a ruched pole. Fabric surrounding the mirror creates a "soft sculpture" effect. To enhance the tone-on-tone feeling and to camouflage imperfect plaster, the raised areas of the walls have been deftly sponged.

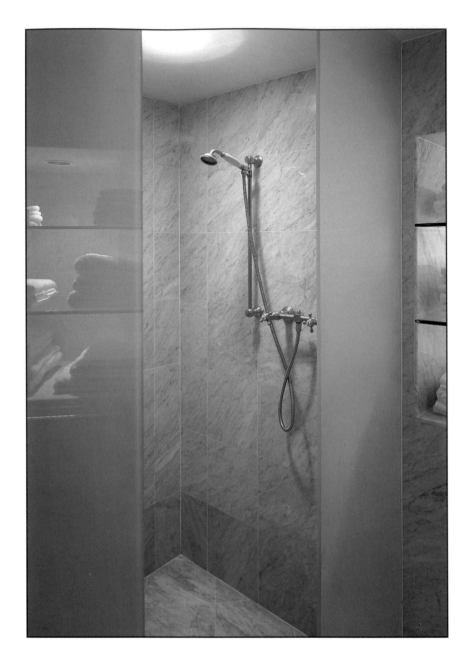

Below: In the small bathroom of a city apartment, the awkward placement of piping is cleverly overcome. A widened windowsill makes up for the counter space the small wall-mounted sink lacks. A large medicine cabinet offers more organized storage than a door-fronted vanity. The brushed stainless steel tub enclosure, ridged-glass shower door, and single-handle faucet are sleek sophisticates.

Above: Cool gray marble clads the floor and ceiling of this elegantly austere shower. Thick tempered glass in opalescent blue-green creates the entrance to the generous enclosure. One of the panels has been fitted with ample shelves for storing towels. The adjustable-height showerhead can also be operated as a handheld unit.

Right: A sea green countertop and pale fine-grained wood cabinetry create a postmodern sanctuary for an aesthete. Touch-latch hinging allows for the nearly seamless addition of a recessed medicine cabinet flanked by tube lighting. Other necessities stow away in drawers and behind doors fitted with brushed aluminum pulls. The toilet is discreetly located away from the sink on the other side of this unit.

Above: This delightful bathroom might have looked dowdy had the walls been papered in a pastel floral and its high ceiling simply painted white. Instead, boldly colored wall covering and pleated tenting give the room real character. Two Irish Regency mirrors, corner draperies, and bamboo étagère are fetching embellishments.

Opposite: A pretty painted three-part screen makes a thirties-style bath most exceptional. Screens such as this one are usually expensive and difficult to come by. A similar feeling can be achieved, however, by covering a solid-wood frame screen with fabric. When working, be sure to cover one panel at a time, making sure that no hinges protrude beyond the edge. If the screen is to be visible from both sides, start by covering the back. This way the front's neat edges will conceal the back's unfinished ones.

Chapter Eight

SUNROOMS AND PORCHES

Opposite: Properly cared for over the years, these 1920s wicker pieces show little signs of wear. Sunlight and its drying rays are wicker's most nefarious foes. Once a wicker piece has dried out completely, it generally disintegrates. But if only portions are dry and the vertical reeds that make up the framework are intact, the piece can usually be repaired. Flaking paint is another problem of antique wicker. Scrub off loose paint with a wire brush, using plenty of water. Once the piece is thoroughly dry, seal it with a primer followed by light coats of paint.

Veranda, portico, loggia, lanai. Atrium, greenhouse, conservatory, Florida room. Called by any name, the sunroom or the summer porch is a warm and wonderful place to pass the time.

The porch acts as a summer living room. The sunroom serves as a year-round sanctum. And despite their architectural attributes, whether these be marble columns, spindlework supports, or brick buttresses, both spaces should bow to nature, blurring the boundaries between indoors and out, turning attention away from decorative trappings.

First and foremost, porch and sunroom furnishings should be comfortable and informal, arranged with a free hand. Pieces should also be light enough to be picked up and moved about easily so that the layout never appears forced or contrived and there's always room for another guest. Summer porch furniture in particular should not be overly cumbersome since it is usually moved indoors at the end of each season. Many cast-off furnishings can work together on a porch or in a sunroom, provided the pieces are painted the same color. Using just one or two fabrics here also unifies the space and keeps it looking fresh and unfussy. Preshrunk cotton and cotton/linen blends make good choices for seat cushions. Washable and more resistant to fading than synthetics, these "naturals" are soft and pliable yet have enough heft to stand up to a high degree of wear and tear. Remember that the tighter the weave, the more durable the fabric. It's also a good idea to stick with simple patterns and colors that are mere foils for flowers and foliage. Materials that are bright and busy can subdue the view and interfere with the restful mood that's so much desired.

Windows and indoor heating are the basic elements that distinguish a sunroom from a summer porch. Sunroom windows should be not only attractive but, if possible, functional and energy-efficient, too. Operable sashes as well as doors should be weather-stripped to minimize heat loss.

Installing new low-e windows will keep the space warmer in the winter and cooler in the summer. In colder climates, a sunroom with no basement underneath can benefit from a hot-water heating system that features plastic piping embedded in its concrete foundation, coupled with conventional radiators at floor level. Toes will indeed stay toasty even in the dead of winter.

Besides structural components, porches and sunrooms also diverge in the ways they are used. Sunrooms are spaces for many practical pursuits. But picture a porch and other images spring to mind: a cool shady shelter from the heat, a haven from sudden summer storms, a front and center seat for watching the sun's slow descent. The porch by its very nature is less utilitarian, more ephemeral than the sunroom. Perhaps that's why whimsical accessories like hammocks and swings are so well suited to it. Fair weather or foul, it's safe to say that together porches and sunrooms provide the best of both worlds.

Opposite: A mismatched grouping of antique wicker furniture adorned with chintz throw pillows lends a casual country air to this tiny urban terrace. The retro-style tablecloth festooned with fruit is purposefully funky. Mounted to the patio's perimeter wall, lattice fencing enhances the sense of privacy. Lattice, in wood or polyvinyl, can be purchased at many garden supply stores and has many ingenious uses for interiors and exteriors alike.

Left: Deep green wicker is a perennially popular choice for porch furnishings—it blends admirably with the natural materials that surround it as well as with the greenery of the landscape. On this airy porch, a heavy chest anchors the grouping and serves as a place to set drinks and stash pillows and throws when stormy weather threatens. Because this porch has no railings, it has a more open feel than those bound by walls or balusters. Emulate this look only if your porch is close to ground level.

Left: Not every flea market find should be scraped, then painted or refinished. The peeling layers of the old wooden table, the wicker settee, and the chairs clad in hues of kitchens from the thirties all contribute to the charm of this sunroom's faded gentility. A spotless background, however, is required to make this look work. Freshly painted walls and new vinyl flooring prevent shabby chic from looking just plain shabby. The window seat and its pillows, in crisp, light hues, possess even more spotless appeal. Adding to the eclectic mix are an elaborate chandelier filched from a formal dining room, pieces of a favorite tea set, and rustic, handcrafted baskets.

Above: Besides being a place to read and relax, almost every sunroom is also a conduit to the lawn or garden. What's more, food and beverages are consumed here frequently. For these reasons, low-maintenance flooring in the sunroom is a must. Sheet vinyl with custom diamond insets and border has been selected for this space. Crimson, awning-striped fabric and a companion floral echo the tone of the beaded-board ceiling. Roman blinds in deep forest green ring the room.

Above: An apartment dweller, deprived of porch and terrace, takes advantage of a sunny corner created by two tall and elegant windows. A passion for painted and idiosyncratic furnishings is more than apparent here. The Victorian recamier has coquille-shaped ends; the rattan breakfast tray shares similar swirling lines. A stout three-drawer with an unusual shape blooms with cabbage roses as does the plump pillow poised for use as a backrest.

Opposite: Lush with a profusion of tropicals, this spacious conservatory recalls the Victorian love of the exotic. Accents brought back from travels abroad mix with animal-print textiles to create a sunroom that is as stunning as it is practical. Weathered brick prevents worries about the floor being stained by an overflow of water and soil from plants. Latticework laid atop the roofing structure lets in the generous sunlight that plants thrive on while subtly filtering rays.

Above: Antique wicker, especially in the elaborate Victorian styles popularized by Wakefield Rattan Co. and Heywood Bros., has become exceedingly expensive. Many wonderful reproductions, however, are now available. With their rattan reeds left natural, the pieces shown here blend beautifully with the pink brick of the patio's wall and floor. Painted pieces, including two birdcages and an old chest, contribute smatterings of color.

Above: Although its structure is similar to that of a folly, this sunroom is exquisitely practical; because of its energy-efficient insulation it can be used year-round. Transom-topped French windows open to capture each garden breeze. In the evening, the gossamer curtains hung from brass rings and poles are drawn for privacy. It's then that the porcelain chandelier suspended from the vaulted, beaded-board ceiling casts its romantic glow.

Above: In the heat of the day this small anteroom feels blissfully cool thanks to its position under a shady porch. Its stucco walls, ragged a periwinkle blue, also psychologically lower the temperature. Trappings—including the dining chairs, the water jar, and the serape used to cover the bench cushion—play up the Mexican motif. The window is sweetly outfitted with iron grille-work and painted "shutters"; the shelf below recalls a window box, walking the line between indoors and out.

Above: The soothing rhythm of its swing sets the measured style of this Southwestern porch. Designed with readers in mind, the swing proffers down-stuffed pillows along its rattan back, and a clever canvas pocket holds books and magazines. Old lengths of a weathered fence make up the porch's railing; red and yellow capitals perch atop porch supports painted turquoise to match the floor. These colors appear again in the freehand banding on the stucco wall.

Left: What better place for a siesta than this small, shady backyard porch. Cool, terra-cotta tiles clad its floor; Mission tiles ripple across its roof. A variety of plantings make this spot even more pleasant.

Right: A deck should marry well with the architecture of a house and also respect its site. This second-floor structure does both, even permitting a tree to thrust skyward through the cedar floor that has silvered to nearly the same hue as its bark. The rail is an important element of this deck's design. Its simple, clean lines offer comely contrast to the flourishes of the reproduction Victorian wicker furniture. Plaid cushions and throw pillows and a braided rug give this space the comfort of a family room transported out-of-doors.

Above: Flagstones in red, blue, and gray tones prompted the colorful and eclectic furniture selection for this porch. An old Adirondack chair has been whimsically painted. The rocket rocker, a relic from the early sixties, remains untouched. Trellises trained with old-fashioned climbing roses offer another glance backward.

Above: When the party is in full swing, sliding doors turn this porch into an extension of the living room as well as an impromptu dance floor. Custom-crafted of oak and glass, the doors exemplify marvelous postmodern design. When the mood is mellow, the porch resumes its purpose as a shady spot for reading or relaxing.

Left: Like the prow of a small, capable sailboat, this tiny porch thrusts instinctively forward. Created to provide shade, the porch, with its rafter trussing and postmodern decorative elements, resembles a two-story dormer, adding interest to the profile of the house. A swing suspended from the rafters and an Adirondack chair provide seating. Adjoining sunny patio space offers an alternative for sun worshipers.

Sources

APPLIANCES

Amana Refrigeration, Inc.
Amana, IA 52204
(800) 843-0304

Bosch
2800 S. 25th Ave.
Broadview, IL 60153
(800) 866-2022

Dacor
950 S. Raymond Ave.
Pasadena, CA 91105
(818) 799-1000

Frigidaire
6000 Perimeter Dr.
Dublin, OH 43017
(800) FRIGIDAIRE

Gaggenau USA
425 University Ave.
Norwood, MA 02062
(617) 255-1766

Garland Commercial Industries
185 E. South St.
Freeland, PA 18224
(717) 636-1000

GE Appliances
AP3-232
Louisville, KY 40225
(800) 626-2000

KitchenAid
(800) 422-1230

Russell Range
3325 S. Maple Ave. #5
South San Francisco, CA 94080
(415) 873-0105

Sub-Zero Freezer Co.
P.O. Box 44130
Madison, WI 53744-4130
(800) 532-7820

Thermador
P.O. Box 22129
Los Angeles, CA 90040
(800) 735-4328

Traulsen
114-02 15th Ave.
College Point, NY 11356
(718) 463-9000

U-Line
P.O. Box 23220
Milwaukee, WI 53223
(414) 354-03300

Viking Range Corp.
111 Front St.
P.O. Drawer 966
Greenwood, MS 38930
(601) 455-1200

Whirlpool Corp.
200 M-63N
Benton Harbor, MI 48009
(800) 235-1301

Wolf Range Co.
19600 S. Alameda St.
Compton, CA 90221-6291
(310) 637-3737

BATHROOM AND KITCHEN FIXTURES AND FAUCETS

American Standard
1 Centennial Plaza
Piscataway, NJ 08855-6820
(800) 524-9797

Elkay Manufacturing
2222 Camden Ct.
Oak Brook, IL 60521
(708) 574-8484

Franke
212 Church Rd.
N. Wales, PA 19454
(800) 626-5771

Grohe America Inc.
241 Covington Dr.
Bloomingdale, IL 60108
(708) 582-7711

Hansa America
1432 W. 21st St.
Chicago, IL 60608
(312) 733-0025

Hansgrohe Inc.
2840 Research Park Dr.
Suite 100
Soquel, CA 95073
(800) 334-0455

Jacuzzi Whirlpool Bath
P.O. Drawer J
Walnut Creek, CA 94596
(510) 938-7070

Jado Bathroom & Hardware Mfg. Corp.
4690 Calle Quetal
Camarillo, CA 93012
(805) 482-2666

Kohler Co.
444 Highland Dr.
Kohler, WI 53044
(800) 4-KOHLER

Moen, Inc.
25300 Al Moen Dr.
North Olmsted, OH 44070
(216) 962-2000

Porcher
6615 W. Boston St.
Chandler, AZ 85226
(800) 359-3261

CABINETS

KraftMaid
16052 Industrial Pkwy.
Middlefield, OH 44062
(800) 654-3308

Merillat
Dept. 5417
P.O. Box 1949
Adrian, MI 49221
(800) 624-1250 Ext. 5417

Plain & Fancy Custom Cabinetry
P.O. Box 519
Schaefferstown, PA 17088
(717) 949-6571

Robern
1648 Winchester Rd.
Bensalem, PA 19029
(800) 877-2376

Rutt
1564 Main St.
P.O. Box 129
Goodville, PA 17528
(215) 445-6751

Smallbone
A & D Building
150 E. 58th St.
New York, NY 10155
(212) 935-3222

Timberlake Cabinet Co.
(800) 722-1510

Wood-Mode Cabinetry
1 Second St.
Kreamer, PA 17833
(717) 374-2711

CARPETING, FLOORING, AND TILE

American Olean
1000 Cannon Ave.
Lansdale, PA 19446-0271
(215) 855-1111

Ann Sacks Tile & Stone
500 NW 23rd Ave.
Portland, OR 97210
(503) 331-7320

Armstrong World Industries
P.O. Box 8022
Plymouth, MI 48170-9948
(800) 704-8000

Bruce Hardwood Floors
Marketing Dept. TZ1-5
16803 Dallas Pkwy.
Dallas, TX 75245
(800) 722-4647

Couristan
2 Executive Dr.
Fort Lee, NJ 07024
(800) WE-LUV-RUGS

Dal-Tile
7834 Hawn Fwy.
Dallas, TX 75217
(800) 933-TILE

Hastings Tile & Il Bagno Collection
30 Comerical St.
Freeport, NY 11520
(516) 379-3500

Karastan Carpets
P.O. Box 12070
Calhoun, GA 30703
(800) 234-1120

Mannington Resilient Floors
P.O. Box 30
Salen, NJ 08079
(609) 935-3000

Masland Carpets
P.O. Box 11467
Mobile, AL 36671
(334) 675-9080

Mohawk Carpets
P.O. Box 12069
Calhoun, GA 30703
(800) 241-4494

S&S Carpet Mills
200 Howell Dr.
Dalton, GA 30721
(800) 241-4013

Stark Carpet Corp.
979 Third Ave.
New York, NY 10021
(212) 752-9000

FANS AND FIREPLACES

Broan Mfg.
P.O. Box 140
Hartford, WI 53027-0140
(800) 558-1711

Casablanca Fan Co.
450 N. Baldwin Park Blvd.
City of Industry, CA 91746

Heatilator Inc.
1915 W. Saunders St.
Mt. Pleasant, IA 52641
(800) 843-2848

Heat-N-Glo Fireplace Products, Inc.
6665 W. Highway 13
Savage, MN 55378
(800) 669-HEAT

Hunter Fan Co.
2500 Frisco, TN 38114
(901) 743-1360

FURNITURE

Avery Boardman
979 Third Ave.
New York, NY 10022
(212) 688-6611

Drexel Heritage
101 N. Main St.
Drexel, NC 28619
(800) 916-1986

Ethan Allen
P.O. Box 1966
Danbury, CT 06813-1966
(800) 228-9229

Grange Furniture, Inc.
200 Lexington Ave.
New York, NY 10016
(212) 685-9494

Henredon
P.O. Box 70
Morganton, NC 28655
(704) 437-5261

Herman Miller for the Home
8500 Byron Rd.
Zeeland, MI 49464
(800) 646-4400

J.G. Stickley
P.O. Box 480
Manlius, NY 13104
(315) 682-5500

Lexington Furniture
P.O. Box 1008
Lexington, NC 27293
(800) LEX-INFO

Thomasville Furniture
P.O. Box 339
Thomasville, NC 27361-0339
(800) 225-0265

HARDWARE

Baldwin Brass
841 E. Wyomissing Blvd.
Reading, PA 19612
(610) 777-7811

Belwith-Keeler
4300 Gerald R. Ford Pkwy.
Grandville, MI 49468-0127
(800) 453-3537

Renovators Supply
P.O. Box 25115
Conway, NH 03818-2515
(800) 659-2211

Restoration Hardware
Koch Service Rd., Suite J
Corte Madera, CA 94925
(415) 924-1005

LIGHTING

Cooper Lighting
400 Busse Rd.
Elk Grove Village, IL 60007
(800) 323-8705

Frederick Cooper, Inc.
2445 W. Diversey Ave.
Chicago, IL 60647
(312) 384-0800

Juno Lighting
P.O. Box 5065
Des Plaines, IL 60017-5065
(708) 827-9880

George Kovacs
67-25 Otto Rd.
Glendale, NY 11385
(718) 629-5201

Lightolier Inc.
100 Lighting Way
Secaucus, NJ 07096
(201) 864-3000

Luxo
36 Midland Ave.
Port Chester, NY 10573
(800) 222-5896

Period Lighting Fixtures
167 River Rd.
Clarksburg, MA 01267
(413) 664-7141

The Stiffel Co.
(312) 664-9200

PAINT

Benjamin Moore Paint Co.
51 Chestnut Rd.
Montvale, NJ 07645
(800) 826-2623

Devoe Paint
P.O. Box 7600
Louisville, KY 40257-0600
(502) 897-9861

Dutch Boy Paints
101 Prospect Ave.
Cleveland, OH 44115
(800) 828-5669

The Glidden Co.
925 Euclid Ave.
Cleveland, OH 44115
(800) 663-8589

Pratt & Lambert Paints
P.O. Box 22
Buffalo, NY 14240
(800) 289-7728

Sherwin Williams Co.
101 Prospect Ave.
Cleveland, OH 44115
(800) 4-SHERWIN

SURFACING MATERIALS

Avonite
1945 Hwy. 304
Belen, NM 87002
(800) 428-6648

Bomanite
P.O. Box 599
Madera, CA 93639-0599
(800) 854-2094

Corian Products
DuPont Co.
PPD Dept.
Wimington, DE 19898
(800) 4-CORIAN

Formica Corp.
10155 Reading Rd.
Cincinnati, OH 45241
(800) FORMICA

International Paper
Nevamar Decorative Surfaces
8339 Telegraph Rd.
Odenton, MD 21113-1397
(800) 777-7888

Wilsonart
(800) 710-8846

**RETAIL HOME FURNISHINGS
AND ACCESSORIES**

Crate & Barrel
725 Landwehr Rd.
Northbrook, IL 60065
(800) 323-5461

IKEA U.S.
496 W. Germantown Pike
Plymouth Meeting, PA 19462
East Coast: (412) 747-0747
West Coast: (848) 912-1119

Laura Ashley Home Collection
1300 MacArthur Blvd.
Mahwah, NJ 07430
(800) 223-6917

Pierre Deux
870 Madison Ave.
New York, NY 10021
(800) 8-PIERRE

Pottery Barn
P.O. Box 7044
San Francisco, CA 94120-7044
(800) 922-5507

Ralph Lauren Home Collection
1185 Ave. of the Americas
New York, NY 10036
(212) 642-8700

WINDOWS AND DOORS

Andersen Windows, Inc.
P.O. Box 70
Brockton, MA 07403
(800) 426-4261

Marvin Windows and Doors
P.O. Box 100
Warroad, MN 56763
(800) 346-5128

Pella Corp.
102 Main St.
Pella, IA 50129
(800) 84-PELLA

Pozzi Wood Windows
P.O. Box 5249
Bend, OR 97708
(800) 821-1016

INDEX

PHOTOGRAPHY CREDITS

© William Abranowicz: 60, 95; Design, Victoria Hagan: 39 left; Design, Tim Haynes and Kevin Roberts: 2 top left, 25, 38, 85; Design, Lee Mindel: 40, 115, 120 both, 121; Design, Ron McCoy: 56, 69; Design, Charles Bumgardner and Mark Chandler for McKenzie-Childs: 165 right; Design, Lee Mindel, Shelton Mindel Associates: 23; Susanna Moore: 110; Design, Carmelo Pomodoro: 2 top right, 41, 64, 119 bottom, 136

© Feliciano: 140; Design, Anthony Child: 8; Design, Howard Graff: 61; Design, Carol Moscey, Interiors: 83; Design, Lyn Peterson: 58 right; Design, Carleton Varney: 71 right

© Mick Hales: Design, Alexander Baer: 49; Design, Dan Carithers: 32

© Tria Giovan: 94, 116, 141 right, 151 left, 156; Stylist, Anita Calero: 36, 72, 131, 150, 151 right, 161; Stylist, Cathy Cook: 37, 59; Design, Stanley Hura: 34; Design, Maia Javan: 57, 129; Design, Sarah Kaltman: 169 right, 170; Design: Kling/ Wright: 84; Design, Patti O'Shaughnessy: 38, 111; Design, Gandy Peace: 104; Design, Charles Riley: 30, 33 top, 47, 54, 58 left, 66, 114, 117 top, 126 both, 127, 135, 141 left, 145, 162, 165 left, 167 left; Architect, Tom Sansone: 86; Design, Anna Thomas: 133

© image/dennis krukowski: Design, Aubergine Interiors, Ltd.: 62 left; Design, David Eugene Bell, A.S.I.D.: 27 left, 98; Design, Sam Botero and Associates.: 50, 154; George Constant, Inc.: 155; Design, Justine Cushins: 124; Antiques, Nancy Frierberg, Connecticut: 26, 128 bottom; Design, Richard Gruber: 144 left; Design, Mark Hampton Inc.: 22; Design, Kevin Lally: 42; Design, Tonin MacCallum A.S.I.D., Inc.: 11, 14, 20, 27 right, 63, 134, 144 right, 163 right; Design, Nancy Mannucci, A.S.I.D.: 15; Design, Ned Marshall Inc.: 35; Design, Libby Cameron for Parish-Hadley Associates, Inc.: 163 left; Design, Gary Jay Paul Architecture & Decorating: 70, 74; Design, Rolf Seckinger Inc.: 48 left; Design, Matthew Patrick Smyth Inc.: 149

© Michael Mundy: Design, A. Penny: 39 right; Design, Dawn Steel LA.: 158

© Eric Roth: 53

© Tim Street-Porter: Design, Anderson: 78, 168 right; Design, Rachel Ashwell: 164; Decorator, Barbara Barry: 44 right, 71 left, 76, 96, 97 right, 100 left, 102, 107 left; Design, Andrew Batey: 139; Design, Tom Beeton: 130; Design, Tom Calloway: 52, 79 left; Architect, David Conner: 79 right; Design, Tony Duquette: 166; Decorator, Waldo Fernandez: 19, 117 bottom; Design, Greene and Greene: 31, 100 right; Grounds, Kent Architects: 147; Design, Jarrett Hedborg: 21 right, 28, 44 left, 77, 86 left, 106, 132, 168 left, 171 left; Design, Hodgetts-Fung: 90; Design, Kathryn Ireland: 24 right; Design, Scott Johnson: 87, 103, 105, 146 right; Design, Debra Jones: 12, 62 right, 92, 97 left, 118; Design, Annie Kelly: 10, 73, 101, 169 left; Design, Hulton W. Kinson: 128 top; Design, Konig/Eizenberg: 107 right, 171 right; Design, Russ Leland: 91; Design, David Ming Lowe: 67; Design, McCormick Interiors: 16; Design, Ron Meyers: 48 right, 108; Design, Moore/Rubel/ Yudell: 18; Design, Brian Murphy: 24 left, 51 right, 88 left, 89, 119 top, 143, 148, 152 left; Design, Ken Payson: 68; Design, Sussman Prezsa: 17; Design, Riley: 82; Design, Parkin Saunders: 33 bottom; Design, Richard Sherman: 80; Design, Claudia Swimmer: 159; Design, Joseph Terrell: 46 bottom; Design, Jeffrey Tohl: 81; Design, Larry Totah: 2 bottom left, 45, 142; Design, Peter Weller: 146 left; Decorator, Hutton Wikinson: 128 top; Design, Allee Willis: 99; Design, Zanuck: 167 right

© Paul Warchol: Stamberg Aferiat Architecture: 2 bottom right, 6, 46 top, 51 left, 65, 122, 152 right; Francoise deMenil Architect: 21 left, 153; Roger Ferri: 88 right; Hariri & Hariri Architects: 43 left; Haverson/Rockwell Architecture: 109, 123 both; Mayers & Schiff Architects: 160 right; Rosenblum/Harb Architects: 160 left